In Praise of Roses

Above: Vagabonde and a new yellow rose from Tantau, Sunblest

Overleaf: In my garden.

On the jacket: Manuela, King's Ransom and Super Star.

Late note

Two new roses from Tantau were named after the text of this book went to press. Their captions are correct on the colour illustrations but are different in the text. Sunblest (above) is referred to in the indexes as Golden Times, and Oriana (plate 35) is called in both text and indexes Tantau's 6446.

Harry Wheatcroft

In Praise of Roses

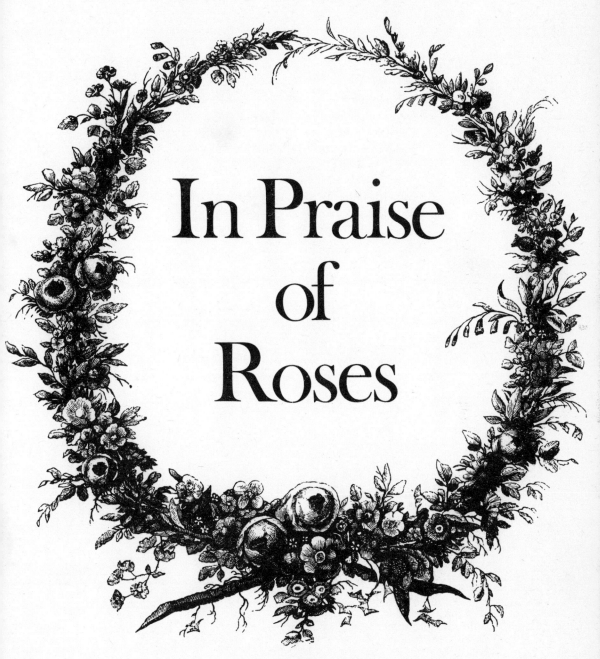

Barrie & Jenkins

I should like to acknowledge the help given by my old friends Mathias Tantau and Willi Kordes in clearing up several points of detail. I am also grateful to the following for their help in providing illustrations: the Royal National Rose Society; Mr Crowson of J. E. Downward; Mr Graham Thomas; Mr Gordon Rowley; my son David; Mr Walter Gregory; Mr R. J. Corbyn; Mr P. W. Harkness.

First published 1970 by
Barrie & Jenkins Ltd
2 Clement's Inn, London WC2
Printed in Great Britain
Type set by
Gloucester Typesetting Co, Ltd, Gloucester
Printed by
Lowe and Brydone Ltd
Victoria Road, London
Colour printing by
D. H. Greaves Ltd, Scarborough
Bound by Leighton-Straker Bookbinding Co Ltd
Standard Road, London NW10

SBN 257.65144.6

Contents

*Bold figures in the margin refer to
the colour plates*

Index to Colour Plates

Arranging my stand at a Royal National Rose
Society show.

Introduction

Books about roses are almost as many, and as diverse, as roses themselves. They range from scholarly tomes of botany through to simple booklets on how-to-do-it. In this book I have not attempted to compete with any of those.

So this is not intended as a primer of instruction. Enough words have already been written about how roses should or should not be grown; it is unnecessary for me to add extensively to them, or to multiply the many different schools of thought which already confuse the rose grower. Certainly this is not a history book, neither is it an autobiography. Better, I think, to describe it as notes on a love affair, an account of one man's romance with the first lady of flowers.

For fifty years or more I have been devoted to roses and have tried to serve them to the best of my ability; first, in partnership with my late brother Alfred, the original team of Wheatcroft Brothers (which remains a separate and independent firm though I am no longer connected with it), then later with my sons David and Christopher in business as Harry Wheatcroft and Sons. When it was suggested that I pass on the benefit of my experience to a still wider circle, I readily agreed.

That is why, now, with my budding knife stored away for the winter, I have taken to a pen—a different sort of propagating tool and one I am far less practised with.

It would be idle to pretend that in this half-century of devotion, there have not been disappointments. But there have been many more triumphs and above all there has been pleasure and excitement abounding. I am a lucky man to have played my part in the development of the rose during the fifty years in which she has made her greatest progress. Now I can look back with pride and pleasure on my contribution to that development, and on my friendship with other rose-raisers in Europe, America, Australasia, and right across the world to Japan. Everywhere, indeed, where men make gardens, I have found friends and colleagues united in working with and for roses.

This introduction was written last, and looking over the assembled manuscript I can see that the effect is something of a patchwork. An offering, someone said, as distinctive as one of my workaday shirts. But this is my book, made in my way; a devotee's tribute to the flower which was once the rich man's treasure but is now everyone's darling.

I have written for everyone, novice or veteran, who is interested in roses, but for the more experienced growers I now suggest an immediate pass into the next chapter. Skip the rest of this one and then read on.

For the inexperienced grower, or the casual reader unversed in the technical terms of the practice, I present a non-alphabetical mini-glossary of what we mean by buds and stocks and hybrid teas and floribundas—some of the words in the rose-man's language when he is talking about either propagation or classification—translated into the simplest terms.

First, the terms used to describe methods of propagating existing varieties.

Bud. This can of course mean the developing flower, but the more technical use of the word is for the embryo shoots, or 'eyes', found at the base of each leaf. If these are removed from their parent plant and subsequently inserted beneath the bark of briar 'stocks' (see below), they go on to grow into rose trees exactly the same as the parent. This operation is called 'budding' and is carried out by commercial growers in order to multiply a few expensively raised parent plants into thousands growing cheerfully on their host stock. Practically all rose trees sold have been budded in

Stick of a cultivated variety showing budding eyes.

Preparing the bud.

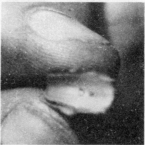

The bud ready for insertion, with the pith removed, and showing the vital centre of the eye from which the growth will spring.

Making the T-cut in the stem of the briar stock, into which the bud will be inserted.

Inserting the bud in the stock.

The bud inserted in the stock.

The inserted stock bound with a rubber band, through which the eye will grow.

this way and on the plant a knob will be seen where the union has been made. Completely new varieties have of course to be raised from seed (see Hybridising).

Budwood, or *scion*, is the stem of the cultivated variety (called a *cultivar*) from which the eyes are taken for insertion into the stock.

Stock. Stocks are the briars, propagated in millions, either from seeds or from cuttings, which are planted out in the rose fields in the autumn (the fall, in the more poetic American usage) or in Spring. The following summer the budders—the people engaged in inserting the tiny bud shoots into the briar stems—go to work. Stocks, now usually of commercially selected strains with various identifying names, are in Europe and America, usually variations of the wild dog rose, *rosa canina* although *rosa multiflora*, another species, is sometimes used to impart more vigour to the budded stock. *Rosa rugosa*, a very spiny species originating in Japan, is the stock now commercially used for most 'standard' roses (see below), or 'tree-roses' as they are called in the United States. (In Britain the word 'tree' is commonly used to describe any mature rose plant.) In countries with particular climatic conditions, such as Africa and India, stocks of native species are mostly preferred as foster-parents for the cultivated rose.

Grafting is another way of propagating. A complete section of the stem of the cultivated variety is joined to the stem of the stock by matching transverse cuts, and the join securely bound so that the two parts of the union will knit together.

Cuttings are hard-wood stems of a plant, cut immediately below a bud, and inserted into a prepared rooting medium (usually containing a high proportion of sand), the object being to make them develop their own roots and grow on to full-sized plants.

Now, the terms used to describe the most creative and exciting aspect of the rose-grower's trade—developing completely new varieties.

Hybridising. This is cross-breeding, the operation of raising a new variety of rose from seed. The seeds are contained in the heps—the

A handful of stocks ready to be planted in the fields.

A field of stocks. Every plant in it will be budded with a cultivated variety.

A rose tree before planting. The 'knob', the union of the stock and the cultivated variety, is just above the roots and shown in a ring.

Buds protected from accidental pollination.

Pollen shaken from a fully open flower lies on the petals.

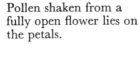

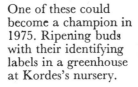

One of these could become a champion in 1975. Ripening buds with their identifying labels in a greenhouse at Kordes's nursery.

A ripe bud just before its seeds are collected.

The first blooms of new seedling varieties. Their original companions in the seed boxes have already been thrown away as unworthy of further propagation.

seed-pods which form after the flower dies. They are, as it were, the fruit of the plant, so of course can appear only after the female part of the plant has been fertilised by pollen from the male. Nowadays fertilisation is a strictly controlled and documented operation, with parent plants carefully chosen to produce a particular characteristic in the resulting 'cross' or hybrid. Old-time growers often left fertilisation to chance, to the efforts of such natural agents as bees or moths. Now it is done by the dab of a pollen-touched camel-hair brush on to selected blooms which have previously been emasculated by removing the male, pollen-bearing parts of the flower (the anther), leaving only the female, pollen-receiving parts (the stigma). Strict control is exercised to prevent any unwanted pollen from accidentally falling, or being deposited by a bee, on to the treated flower.

The seed, when ripened, is sown in a greenhouse in sandy compost and may take up to a year to germinate. But eventually the seedling plant grows and bears flowers which give the hybridiser his first chance to see whether his care has resulted in something new and beautiful—or in an ugly duckling no one will want. If the first test is passed, tiny eyes from the seedling plant are budded on to small briar stocks, so that the new variety can be tested under field conditions. In Britain the Royal National Rose Society's trial grounds at St. Albans are often used for these tests. Selection, re-selection—but most often rejection—follow over the subsequent years. If the rose is considered good enough, it will finally find its way into commerce five years or more from the time it first sprouted its seedling leaves.

32

Pollen parent is the term used to describe the variety employed to fertilise the new cross—the father, as it were. *Seed parent* is the term for the variety on to which the pollen was introduced for the development of the seed—in other words, the mother plant.

Sport. A sport is a natural variation from the norm—a mutation —as for instance, in a bush variety which suddenly shows climbing tendencies, or in a change of colour. If the sport looks promising, stem-buds from the shoot which has sported may be used to establish this natural mutation as a new variety in its own right.

A *maiden* is a rose tree up to twelve months old. *Maiden growth* is that made in the first year.

Cut back. After their maiden year, trees are severely pruned or 'cut back'.

Now for the terms used to describe the different types of roses.

Hybrid Tea, Floribunda, Tea, Hybrid Perpetual. Groups into which our modern roses are classified, according to their habits and ancestry.

The pure tea roses, usually extremely susceptible to frost and intolerant of anything but first-class growing conditions, were evolved first. Then came the hybrid perpetuals, a hardier race claimed, hence the name, to be more persistently flowering than their forebears. Neither teas nor hybrid perpetuals, though, were anything like so persistent in flowering as most roses in our gardens today. Very few varieties of tea or hybrid perpetual remain in cultivation.

Crosses between teas and hybrid perpetuals gave us the modern hybrid teas. Lastly came the modern floribunda, which developed from the small, often single-flowered varieties of its earlier days into the near-hybrid tea sized blooms which many carry today. So strongly has this propensity for fewer, bigger flowers been developed among latter day floribundas that it is difficult now, even for the expert, to state definitely into which category certain varieties belong. Paddy McGredy, Charm of Paris, Blessings and Pink Supreme are typical 'in betweens'.

Essentially the hybrid teas carry bigger flowers, fewer to the stem, than the orthodox floribundas. Moreover there is generally a perceptible lapse of time between the crops of flowers. Floribundas should be almost continuous-flowering, with new flowering shoots breaking from a lower eye even before the previous crop of blooms is finished. The penalty for growing some of the larger-flowered floribundas is that they perceptibly fail in this.

Because the existing classifications are becoming relatively blurred, there are moves now afoot to evolve a completely new classification for rose types and this may be the only answer to a 'which is what' problem that confuses gardeners all over the world.

A typical hybrid tea.
This is Pink Peace.

A typical 'In-between'
hybrid tea and flori-
bunda. Paddy McGredy
is shown.

A typical Floribunda.
In this case, City of
Belfast.

A standard. This happens to be an eighty-year-old
specimen of Mme Caroline Testout.

A weeping standard. This is Excelsa.

Super Star

Queen Elizabeth

Grandiflora is not a name with any botanical basis. It is applied, largely in America, to the taller growing floribundas with very large flowers, almost hybrid tea-like in size, such as Queen Elizabeth and Roundelay. The term is not officially recognised by the Royal National Rose Society.

Standard roses (tree roses) are obtained by budding the chosen variety (it can be hybrid tea or floribunda) on to briar stocks at a much higher level than normal—about three feet six inches from the ground.

Weeping standards, with long, down flowing, domed heads of bloom, can only be obtained by budding climbing varieties, and even here the choice is extremely restricted, since only varieties with long, lax stems, such as Dorothy Perkins, Excelsa, Albertine, or more preferably the persistent-flowering The New Dawn, can be trained to the proper shape.

Which leads, inevitably, to the question: What is the difference between a *climbing rose* and a *rambler*?

You will find this question answered again later on in the preamble to my chapter listing a selection of climbers. But this little glossary would be even more curtailed if I omitted a word or two about them here.

Both climbers and ramblers of course, climb. But the ramblers, typified by Dorothy Perkins and the similar, scarlet Excelsa, usually have much less rigid stems than climbers and bear only one crop of masses of small flowers each year.

The climbers have much stiffer stems and far fewer canes coming from the base of the plant than ramblers. A *climbing sport* (as explained above) is derived from a mutation of a normal bush variety and therefore tends to bloom only at the top of the plant, as its forebears did. The climbers generally have bigger flowers, though fewer of them to the truss, than ramblers. Many of them produce successive crops of bloom throughout the season, unlike the once-only-flowering ramblers. They come in a range of sizes, some growing to thirty feet, while others stay upright pillar roses only eight feet or so high.

B

A large-flowered climber.
This is Mme Grégoire
Staechelin.

A rambler. This is
Veilchenbläu, mentioned
in the chapter on blue
roses as being still the
bluest rose we have.

Miniature roses, on the other hand, are measured only in inches. They are the little ones, varying between nine and eighteen inches high, which can be grown in troughs or boxes or small flower pots, either indoors or out. Despite their size, they are hardy and with all the characteristics, likes and dislikes, of their bigger cousins. A most delightful way of growing them is in a garden of their own, say some six feet square, divided into mini-beds so that their Lilliputian charms are displayed as though in a model.

Miniatures have been as skilfully bred as the bigger roses. They are propagated by budding, or by grafting, or by cuttings rooted under glass. There is even one variety, listed as *rosa polyantha nana*, which can be treated like an annual and sown from seed, when it will flower with small pale pink heads on fifteen-inch plants, only a few months after being sown. It is strictly a novelty and is useless for bedding, but if you want to try it, look in a seedman's catalogue, not a rose grower's.

Species. This is, strictly, the term employed to describe the original wild varieties. In its wild state the rose is found only in the northern hemisphere, but in countries as far apart as Greenland and Afghanistan. Altogether, there are some 200 known species, but only a few of them are suitable for garden cultivation.

Throughout this book you will find mention of botanical names in Latin and descriptions such as 'hybrid musk'. The botanical names are of species. Such terms as 'hybrid musk' indicate that modern raisers have bred from the species in an attempt to reproduce some desired characteristic of growth, hardiness, colour, or even scent. The chapter on shrub roses explains many of the names.

Shrub roses. A rather loose term used to describe the oldest-known varieties, new ones of free-growing habit and, some climbers which can be allowed to spread naturally. The term 'old roses' is often associated with shrub roses, but properly speaking old roses are those introduced, or growing, before 1900, while there are many shrub roses which have been raised since then and hybridisers continue, thank goodness, to introduce new ones. Species are frequently included in catalogues of shrub roses.

Three bowls of miniature roses.
Compare the size of the cigarette, bottom right.

Single flowered roses are those bearing blooms with one row of five petals only.

Semi double flowers have more than five but not more than fifteen petals.

Double blooms usually contain twenty-five or more petals.

A *full petalled* rose means one of substantial blooms each containing perhaps forty-five or more petals.

The following abbreviations, in common use, have been employed in this book, particularly in the chapters on my selections:

Cl.   —   climbing
Fl.   —   floribunda
Ft   —   feet
H.   —   hybrid
In.   —   inches
HT   —   hybrid tea
PFC —   perpetual flowering climber
R.   —   *Rosa* (denoting a species)
Sh.   —   shrub
Syn. —   synonym (roses often have different names in different countries)
Var. —   variety
×   —   crossed with

The Greatest Roses in My Life

Your job, I was once told, is to pick winners. This sounds as though I was with racing people but in fact I was among a fraternity of rose-breeders, talking over new varieties ready to be launched to the public—each carrying some man's hope of achievement and reward. It was up to me, as number one salesman, to review their efforts: to say 'This one will make the grade and that one won't.'

Would this newcomer, if introduced, become a public hit or would it prove unsaleable, because, pretty as it was, it was just another red floribunda in an age when red floribundas were already a drug on the market? Could I expect the public to ask happily for a rose with a name like Ama Tsu Otome, or even Atom Bomb, eye-catching though this rose from my friend Willi Kordes really was?

These, and many more, are the questions I've had to decide for myself, as over fifty years I've tried to select those roses worth a place in everyone's garden, and to reject the main body of also-rans, those which, even if they came into commercial existence at all, would be bound to fade quickly into obscurity.

Those racing men and I really do have something in common. We both have to study pedigree, performance and form. And, if not horses for courses, then flowers for showers. Some roses, like Karl Herbst, for instance, can be winners in the relatively congenial, mild atmosphere of the south of England; magnificent in the garden, capable at any time on the exhibition bench of taking the award for 'best in show'. But they can fail to make any sort of impact in the wetter, colder north. Montezuma comes into that category. So does Tiffany. And Confidence, hardly aptly named, is capable of producing fine specimen blooms—if it doesn't rain.

Looking back, I suppose I can claim, in my fifty years in the business, to have introduced hundreds of new varieties of roses to gardeners and their gardens. Among them I have had personal favourites—like Belle Blonde, which ultimately failed—and others, **16** like Gold Crown, which have sold out year after year, even though, at first, I had nagging doubts about them. But without hesitation I can name the big four of my time. They are Peace, Super Star, Queen Elizabeth and Fragrant Cloud. Landmark roses, every one, and I travelled the world to find them.

Let me describe one such trip. A visit to Holstein, Germany, which led to the discovery of the gem that was to become Super **3** Star. When I first saw them they were just three plants in an array of some 1,500 to 2,000 new seedlings raised that year by Mathias Tantau, son of a rose-growing father who himself had started hybridising as a schoolboy. There displayed were all the results of Mathias's efforts that year. Beauties galore, set out two varieties to the yard, spread over twenty rows, each 100 yards long. But among all those, shining even from fifty yards away, were these three plants carrying blooms of sparkling salmon-vermilion, a colour break I had never seen before. And I was grey enough in the whiskers to know that this was a real winner.

'You've got a world-beater here,' I told Mathias. But he was cautious.

'We must wait and see. *You* know how many setbacks there can be after a promising start,' he answered. 'My father began this particular cross twenty years ago. Over the years, we have raised 100,000 seedlings carrying this strain—and had to discard them all. Now we have just these three.'

Super Star, blooming in your garden today, may delight you, but remember the frustrating twenty-year quest before it was achieved.

Seven years after I first saw those three seedlings—and that is the time it takes to get a new rose into commercial production after it has shown its first blooms—I was able to exhibit Super Star to the world on our stand at the Royal Horticultural Show at Chelsea.

It went on to win the accolade of a gold medal from the National Rose Society of Great Britain that very year.

Now why should this magnificent, almost iridiscent flower, so splendid a grower, be called Super Star, and not some delightfully feminine name? I am to blame for that. It was just a code number in Mathias Tantau's breeding records at the time I first saw it in his nursery. When it became obvious that this was *the* one after so many years of patient effort, Mathias wanted to call it Ilse Tantau, after his wife who had shared so many of his hopes and failures. 'But that name won't sell over here,' cautioned the Americans. So Mathias reluctantly dropped it. Then someone suggested it should be called Harry Wheatcroft, but I was not having that. 'No, let's call it Super Star,' I suggested. Because here, truly was a new star in the rose firmament, a super one in every way.

The Americans, though, wouldn't go along with even that. 'The Conard Pyle Rose Company here have been using the word Star as a trademark for some time,' they said. 'It would be wrong to market a new rose as Star when it had nothing to do with them.' And that is why Super Star is now known in America as Tropicana. We went ahead happily, all over the rest of the world, with Super Star. And we never hitched our wagon to a brighter one.

There were just those three Super Stars in the world, blooming anonymously in Tantau's garden, when I first saw them. But it was different with Queen Elizabeth. There were thousands, literally thousands, of Queen Elizabeths in existence when I first made that great lady's acquaintance, when she, too, was then still hiding her charms under a trial ground number. Her christening, though, had already been planned.

The variety had been raised by Dr. Walter E. Lammerts, of Livermore, California, a veteran the Americans fondly call 'the father of scientific rose breeding'. He had begun work on it just after the war, crossing Charlotte Armstrong, a tall-growing blood-red hybrid tea of his own breeding, with Floradora, a red floribunda raised by the Tantaus in Germany. And who would have expected the orchid-pink Queen Elizabeth to come from a crossing of two reds?

I had seen Dr Lammerts's new, then unnamed 'grandiflora' as the Americans call it, blooming in various places, some of them

1,000 miles apart, during the nation-wide tour of America that I made in 1952, and nowhere were its orchid-pink blooms more vividly impressive than on the trial ground of Germain's, a firm of distributors on the outskirts of Los Angeles, with which Walter Lammerts was then associated. Queen Elizabeth looked down on you there from stems eight to ten feet high and as thick as young tree trunks.

'What's this rose to be called?' I asked.

'Only this morning,' they said, 'we had permission, through the British Consul, to name it after your queen, Queen Elizabeth.'

I stood silently before the beauty, delighted at so happy a choice of name. For this was indeed a real queen.

'Would you like to distribute it in Britain?' I was asked.

'I'd be honoured.'

'Then we'll send you some plants to be going on with.'

Now the American plants of Queen Elizabeth were all much bigger than anything I have ever seen the variety achieve in this country (and remembering the stature they've reached under Sidney Gault's care in London's Regent's Park that is saying something). In fact, budded on multiflora stocks, which always produce an outsize root system, they were three or four times the size of ours in every way.

'We'll mail them to you first-class,' the Americans said. And I was delighted—until, doing a hasty mental calculation, I realised that forty or fifty bushes, sent air mail, would cost my firm a small fortune in freightage. But there was another shock coming. 'How will 1,000 trees do you, for a start?' I was asked.

'Fine . . . fine. Just fine,' I said dazedly.

They came over in ten crates, each crate measuring five feet by four feet by four feet, a hundred trees to each.

To find the first British home for the new import that spring, we uprooted a thousand trees from the greenhouses where we were preparing our exhibits for the forthcoming Chelsea show. We did not lose one of those 1,000 Queen Lizzies. But we had only a bare handful of her beautiful blooms ready in time for Chelsea that year. A week later we could have shown 100 perfect blooms—and the week after that, 1,000.

We put Queen Elizabeth on the market in 1954 and it went on to win the Rose Society's gold medal; the President's trophy for the best rose of the year—in fact, everything it could win here, as it has done in America, except the Clay Cup for fragrance. For fragrance indeed is all that it lacks. Nearly twenty years after its birth in California, it is still unsurpassed among its kind, the yardstick by which every subsequent grandiflora has been judged.

5   But if we respect this queen for her long reign, what are we to say of Peace, the most famous rose of them all? So much has already been written of this enchanting beauty that I, one of her oldest and most devoted admirers, really have little to add. How she was raised in France, flown to America as a small batch of maiden bushes (under her nursery code number of 3–35–40) as the Germans advanced, and how she took the world by storm after being the centrepiece on every table at the United Nations' Conference at San Francisco in 1945. All that has been told by more compelling pens than mine. Let me merely say, of my acquaintance with the great lady, that I was first to introduce her to Great Britain and that over the years I have sold more specimens of Peace than any other rose. Perhaps a million wouldn't be an overestimate.

In refreshing my memory of the early days of our association, I have just been looking through the Rose Society's Annual of 1948. It contains a report on the first performance of Peace in their trial ground at Hayward's Heath, Sussex—our firm had submitted the required six plants. The judges—and I wasn't one of them in those days—had given her a first-class certificate and an immediate gold medal. And their report had added: 'This is a wonderful rose and will be in great demand.' Never before, never since, have I known such a glowing tribute paid officially to a variety on trial in this country. And those judges have proved the soundest of prophets. For Peace has become the greatest rose best-seller of all time. Not merely here, but throughout the world. Nine years after its introduction, an American authority calculated that there were then some thirty million bushes of Peace growing in every corner of the earth where men had cared to make gardens.

Since then, the number must approximate to 100,000,000—an international share-out of beauty, all from one seed sown, in the first place, in a tiny bed of sandy soil at Lyons in France. And still the demand for Peace goes on, unchecked but not, I trust, unfulfilled. As a nurseryman, I can pay her this tribute, which even I

Three generations of the
Meilland family. First
Antoine (Papa) Meilland
among his seedlings in a
greenhouse at Antibes.
Then his son Francis,
the raiser of Peace, is
shown next to me,
examining new varieties
on the Antibes nursery.
The third generation,
Francis's son Alain, is
shown inspecting new
seedlings.

could not have foreseen when I first introduced her. She is as strong, as full of stamina and vigour today as she was when she was first brought out. In other words—those racing terms again—she's a born stayer.

You see, roses, like other plants raised incessantly by such means as budding and cuttings, inevitably suffer a failing called vegetative degeneration. Which means loss of vigour in succeeding generations, or, more bluntly, just plain old age. But the genuine rose species—the wild roses of the world—are virtually immune from this. And Peace has inherited longevity because she has the blood of one of these species, technically a *Rosa foetida bicolor* seedling, in her immediate pedigree. But that is a technicality. The basic fact, for which you and I and every other rose-lover everywhere should be grateful, is that while others, younger than she, have come, bloomed, boomed, then died out through sheer exhaustion, Peace has stayed as lovely, as young and as vigorous as ever. And unlike some other beauties—Frensham, for instance, which proved sterile —Peace has made her mark as a parent, too.

There has been only one other flushed lemon yellow beauty like her: Grand'mère Jenny, her own daughter. And if you knew the people behind the roses, as I do, and as I hope you will better after reading this book, that fact can give you a quiet chuckle. For Francis Meilland, the man who raised Peace, named it Madame A. Meilland, after his mother. And he raised Grand'mère Jenny, too—and named it after his paternal grandmother. So Grand'mère Jenny is, in fact, Peace's mother-in-law!

Francis Meilland lived only eight years to see the rose world take his two so fondly-named beauties to its heart. But his work and his name live on. Peace ensured that. From the royalties derived from the sale of that supreme variety alone—and new roses were copyright property in America and France long before they were here —the Meillands, it was once estimated, must have made at least £1,000,000. And with it they built themselves a brand new rose-raising empire on the shores of the Mediterranean, on the Cap d'Antibes. There, under ten acres of glass, not to coddle the plants but to make selection easier, they are raising upwards of 100,000 new seedlings every year: who knows but that one of them, one day, may prove another Peace?

6

So to my fourth all-time winner: the intriguing, enchanting Fragrant Cloud. I've told you that when I first saw Super Star on Mathias Tantau's nursery, I noticed its brilliance fifty yards off. This one I smelt, quite literally, half a mile away.

Scent in roses is an elusive quality. It cannot be bred for; it cannot be calculated. The crossing of two highly-scented parents is as likely as not to produce unscented progeny. When scent is there, it's a bonus, an extra prize, a gift from the Gods. Which Fragrant Cloud certainly had that day in Germany, on the same ground where seven or eight years earlier I had found the inestimable Super Star.

For Tantau had been working out breeding lines for Fragrant Cloud, just as he and his father had done for Super Star. An unnamed seedling—unscented, I believe—was one parent; the highly scented Prima Ballerina, an old favourite of mine, the other. Tantau had hoped for another colour break. What he got was a stubby, under medium-sized plant but one full of vigour, capable of producing crop after crop of bloom as freely as any floribunda, and with flowers of an attractive dusky coral shade. But above all Fragrant Cloud, so justly named, had that heady, penetrating, old world perfume. For a second time Mathias Tantau had hit the jackpot. I had half a dozen blooms of it on view in a small vase at the National Rose Society's summer show at Alexandra Palace in 1963, the year it won its gold medal, and another, more fully opened, in my buttonhole. This I kept thrusting forward under the noses of astonished visitors, saying 'Smell this, ladies, smell this.'

They thought I had a nerve. They said 'There's old Harry, at it again'. But I was on to another winner. And I had to keep at it all the time to bring the gems of the world into the gardener's jewel box.

How New Varieties
are Born

Since the breeding of new roses became an industry, instead of the sideline it used to be, it is possible only to guess at the number of new seedlings raised throughout the world every year. A sizeable, concentrated breeding unit—like Meillands, in France; or Jackson and Perkins, or Armstrong and Lindquist in America—each aim to bring a hundred thousand new varieties into existence each season. Multiply their efforts say, by ten; throw in the production of the hundreds of smaller firms, not to mention the amateurs, and I estimate that something like two million tiny seedlings, each a completely brand-new variety, come into being, however briefly, every twelve months.

Roses have entered the conveyor-belt age. The nurseryman of years ago—the people who gave us roses such as La France and Caroline Testout of grandfather's day—would experiment in his lifetime with one or two chance crosses. And, as often as not, forget exactly how he had crossed them. Selling plants was his job; breeding something new was, if he had time for it, his hobby or at best his sideline. But since science and big business took over, the quest for new beauties is now very much a computerised, mass-production job. Like football pool punters, they're even using permutations for their winners today. And it will not be long, I'm sure, before some time-study expert is brought in to report on the work rate of the pollinators. The birds and the bees got the sack long ago!

I suppose, with the rewards to be won from a world-beater in this copyright-protected age, some attempt to turn seed-parents into battery-hens, their progeny to be hatched out in thousands like day-old chicks, was inevitable. But there are snags.

Novelties are the lifeblood of any commercial grower's business. He must sell to live—and a new selling line is always welcome. But how many proven first-class varieties are disappearing today from the catalogues, just to make way for something that can merely be hailed as a 'startling new introduction'? I'm not trying to sound like a prophet of doom, but I would urge my fellow nurserymen and those who plant our products in their gardens to be careful. Never throw out old friends merely to develop almost-unknown new acquaintances. Believe me, some of the roses we've had and which some growers have since discarded, are still so good that those who have dropped them might well hail them all over again, as the ones they have been looking for . . . if only they could come back with new names.

Examples? Oh, there are dozens. Eden Rose, Perfecta, Helen Traubel, Ena Harkness, My Choice, Grand'mère Jenny. I plead guilty over all of those. I've had to keep them off our sales list— merely because our plant despatching complexities are such that if we are to try something new, even just for one season, some old favourite has to be stood down. But inside my own garden, I can please myself, and all those varieties I have mentioned are flourishing at home still, just as rewardingly as when I first planted them.

The culling that goes on in the rearing nurseries is, of course, incessant—and phenomenal. Meilland's 100,000 seedlings, for instance, have a mere four or five survivors left after two years. In their greenhouses I've seen foot-high piles of discarded seedlings, piled up in the aisles as though someone had been conducting a ferocious onslaught on groundsel or some such invading weed. Of the two million new seedlings raised everywhere each year, not more than twenty, I'd say, ever reach commercial production. And only a handful of these will ever be in great demand.

The chances of another Peace or Super Star? Oh, one in every twenty million. In other words, one real world champion every ten years or so—if we're lucky. Now what worries me, with all this mass production, is how many potential champions are being discarded almost at birth; uprooted, consigned to the weed heap, never given a real chance, simply because no one ever happened to see them blooming in their finest hour.

For these little seedlings, growing three inches apart in their specially blended sandy seed-beds—the sandier the better, it helps to facilitate lifting—are, at that stage of their existence, as ephemeral as butterflies. Many may show their real potential for no more than a few fleeting minutes with their first blooms. And, unless they're inspected every half hour—and you can imagine the labour force this would take in ten outsize greenhouses—some new Super Star may easily go undetected, get uprooted as a failure and become lost to the world for ever.

So, with this risk, the whole business of rose-raising, for all its slide-rule efficiency, can still be hit or miss. Mostly miss.

Anyone, it used to be said, can breed a winner. Parsons, clerks, schoolmasters, even income-tax men. They've all been responsible for breeding some of the beauties that have graced our gardens in the years gone by. Ena Harkness, one of the finest roses of our time (note it in the red hybrid tea list) was raised by an amateur, Mr Albert Norman, whose real job, I believe, was connected with diamond cutting in Hatton Garden. But his success with Ena was no fluke, for he also gave us Frensham, for many years the best seller among floribundas, and he later produced Isobel Harkness, Ann Elizabeth, Vera Dalton and others. Quite recently another amateur won a gold medal with the vermilion shrub rose Fred Loads.

But by the end of the 1960s the mathematical chances of an amateur raising a rose which would earn and keep a place in the catalogues had decreased almost to nothing by the overwhelming preponderance of contenders from the concentrated output of the big factory-line raisers. Yet such are the idiosyncrasies of this intriguing business that anyone in fact can *still* breed a winner. Equally, anyone can fail to see when a winner makes its first bow. It took a long time, for instance, for Prima Ballerina to make its mark, as it did for Stella and for Josephine Bruce. Picture was once discarded, then reprieved and put into cultivation to become a universal favourite.

Anna Wheatcroft, that soft salmon floribunda with a perpetual

Fragrant Cloud

At Adolf Horstmann's, the largest retail nursery in Europe

With Mathias and Ilse Tantau

Anna Wheatcroft

Sarabande

Wendy Cussons

Mme Louis Laperrière

Crimson Glory
(*photo Gordon Rowley*)

With Willi Kordes

smile on her face (she bears the name of one of my nieces) is another winner that got a second chance. And I can claim the responsibility or credit, whichever you will, for salvaging this one when it might have ended in the ashes of an autumn bonfire. Anna was raised in Germany by Mathias Tantau some three years before his Super Star was born. Without doubt, it was the result of one of the colour mutations Tantau had hit upon in the development of his masterpiece. There was already an arrangement that Wheatcrofts should market Tantau's introductions in the United Kingdom. As a result of this he was sending us batches of seedlings that he thought promising enough for further limited propagation, so that they could be tried here before their general possibilities were finally assessed. Among them, that year, was the then unchristened seedling, Anna.

At the end of that season—I believe it was 1953—Mathias and I compared notes on how the varieties under test had fared in our two nurseries. When we came to talk about Anna he said: 'No, not that one. It's useless. We're scrapping it here.'

'But my dear Mathias,' I protested, 'You are wrong. Here in Nottingham it is a gem, a jewel. Why, when I visit our testing ground every morning the first variety I make for is this one. It is a never-failing delight.'

So Mathias agreed to go ahead with this delicate (only in colour) soft vermilion, and Anna Wheatcroft came among us. One of her parents was Cinnabar, a floribunda raised by Mathias Tantau's father, and this, in turn, was an offspring of Baby Château, a floribunda produced by a cross between a hybrid musk and a hybrid tea, by that other great German rosarian Willi Kordes just before the war. Baby Château, perhaps because Hitler was so soon to stop rose production throughout Europe, was never the hit Kordes hoped. In fact, he once told me he thought this new fragrant little dark-crimson 'such a disappointment, so unreliable in its flowers.' Yet ask Willi Kordes, the man who has given us so many first-class roses—Crimson Glory, Perfecta, Karl Herbst, Gail Borden, to name only a few—what he considered his greatest achievement and you would be told: 'To have raised Baby Château.' Yes, his once considered flop.

For Baby Château represented years of patient trying on his part, years of effort in search of an ideal. Kordes, you see, had

C

always been fascinated by an old dusky black-crimson hybrid tea called Château de Clos Vougeot, introduced by the illustrious French hybridist Pernet-Ducher in 1908. But it was a donkey to get to grow. Kordes, the rose-growing son of a rose-grower, decided to try to improve on his favourite by a series of crosses. None of them was very impressive but one seedling which itself never saw the light of commercial day was crossed again with the British-raised dark crimson Aroma. And that crossing produced Baby Château. It was a floribunda, not the hybrid tea he'd hoped for, but Kordes called it Baby Château because, to his eternally-hopeful mind, the newcomer at least bore some resemblance to his old favourite.

It was typical of the man, when Baby Château was obviously not going to catch the world's eye, that he decided to try again. He crossed it this time with his already established masterpiece, Crimson Glory. Once more there was disappointment. But even that didn't deter the patient Willi—and then came success. A second generation cross yielded a seedling that was eventually to send the whole rose world into raptures. It was a dark, smouldering geranium in colour—an entirely new break. The first of its generation of the so-called 'hot' colours. Kordes called it Sondermeldung—his 'Special Announcement'. It was sent to the Bagatelle rose trials in Paris and there, in 1943, even while the two countries were still at war, it was awarded a gold medal.

But, 'with Hitler going crazy', as he puts it, Kordes still had to wait years before he could give his new baby to the world. In fact, he waited until 1950. And then it was launched under a new title: Independence. It was a great name for what was then a great introduction. Independence, as I tell you in a later chapter, was so typical of Kordes the man.

But even in this long delayed moment of triumph, he had to suffer yet one more frustration. The Rose Society gave his startling new variety a gold medal in the year of its introduction, but under a wrong name: Cinnabar—that of Anna Wheatcroft's mother; I remember the error well. My firm staged Independence at the Rose Society summer show of 1950, when it got its award. At the same time as we won a gold for Meilland's Grand'mère Jenny and Eden Rose and Kordes's Karl Herbst.

Red Roses

Red roses for romance. Red roses for the inspiration of poets, writers, ballad-composers, artists. For every man in love. Red roses for my lady.

Red roses may be the accepted demonstration of masculine devotion but are they always the treasures of a woman's heart, as enthralled males imagine? I ask because, in my experience, it is men, not women, who buy red roses, be they cut blooms or plants. It is men, not women, who are spell-bound by the red rose. Many a lady among my customers has told me: 'When it comes to choosing the red varieties, Mr Wheatcroft, I leave the selection to my husband. He is much more taken with reds than I am.' And I believe that experience is general among nurserymen.

Man's eyes are on the red, the glamorous dark beauties, and have been ever since the first red rose came to Britain nearly 700 years ago, brought here, it is claimed by Edmund Langley, Duke of Lancaster, son of King Edward I, as a prize of war after a punitive expedition to southern France. *Rosa gallica* that probably was, the same *Rosa gallica* that we grow in shrub gardens today, first captured for Europe by Crusaders returning from the East. Langley's introduction, if we may use a modern phrase, is said to have become the red rose of the House of Lancaster. York's white rose, *Rosa alba*, had been domiciled centuries earlier—it came with the Romans—and together they were to make that mythical hybrid, botanically non-existent, the Tudor Rose of England, the rose of the English kings.

But enough of history. What concerns me more, as I look out on my garden beds of Ena Harkness and Josephine Bruce, and those tall old Dicksons, Hugh and George, is a world-wide effort engaging the attention of rose men of the 1970s—the quest for the perfect, or near-perfect, dark red. For if a fortune awaits the first man to raise a truly blue rose, hardly less, I am sure, will be the reward for the breeder who gives us what we have all been looking for since rose gardens were created: the ultimate in lustrous, dark, bounteously-scented crimsons. Scent it must have. Scent as compelling as the bloom itself. Pinks, yellows, whites, bicolours or blues may all lack it and still be welcomed beauties. But lack of fragrance in a red rose is somehow indefensible. We expect, we demand reds to have scent.

I often think how the present Sam McGredy must have cursed all the vast unseen army of leprachauns, when his red Uncle Walter, in many ways so admirable, opened to reveal the red's greatest deficiency. We could adapt ourselves to Uncle's habit of stretching to the heavens, at least six feet towards them—a trait that is not shown until its second year of growth, and which led the National Rose Society to re-classify it from hybrid tea to shrub— but we cannot even meet it half way over its lack of scent!

I can sympathise, too, with my neighbour Walter Gregory when his Wendy Cussons came deep rose-cerise, instead of the pure red it so easily could have been. Walter has raised many fine roses. Wendy is perhaps the finest of them, though his 1969 introduction Summer Holiday bids fair to run her close. But that, like Wendy, has not the tint to enrapture lovers of a red, red, rose.

Hadley, Hoosier Beauty, Etoile de Hollande, Christopher Stone, Malar Ros, Mardi Gras, Mme Louis Laperrière, Happiness, New Style, Tradition—I have grown them all. Many have been beauties. None has completely satisfied me.

In my experience, Hugh and George Dickson—originally introduced as hybrid perpetuals but now generally accepted as hybrid teas—Crimson Glory, Ena Harkness, Charles Mallerin, Josephine Bruce and Papa Meilland, have all been milestones on the road to progress. But, once again, none of these is the end of that road.

Josephine Bruce.

Walter Gregory.

The Dicksons, like Ena, couldn't hold their heads upright. In botanist's terms, they are afflicted with a weak pedicel, a flower-stalk of insufficient strength to uphold their magnificent flowers. Crimson Glory is but a struggling veteran now. Lazy old Josephine, sprawling over her bed, too often needs revivers and refreshers from the medicine chest, especially to fend off her inherent complaint of mildew, for anyone to reckon *her* one hundred per cent.

I rate Charles Mallerin, raised by Francis Meilland and named after the rival breeder who had taught him so much, as the finest dark red so far—at least for its individual blooms. In colour, deep, wonderful, lustrous dark red; in petal structure, and not least in fragrance, it is as near to perfection as I have yet seen. Alas, it has to be consigned to the ranks of those that promised much and yet failed in the final achievement. For Charles Mallerin, like the modern Uncle Walter twelve years later, developed a peculiarity of growth that rules it out for all but exhibitors of the individual bloom. Whereas Uncle Walter, once its maiden year of growth is over, sends four or five shoots soaring high, Charles Mallerin sends only one. The others dwindle in uncompetitive awe. The result is that a bed of Charles Mallerin looks like an assembly of pencil-written ticks: one small branch and one long and freely-drawn! The exhibitors' rhapsody, the bedding-gardeners' groan.

So what do we need in the near-perfect red, the one guaranteed a place in every nurseryman's list throughout the world? I say we need a rose with the bedding capacities of Ena Harkness, the colour of Charles Mallerin, with all the dark red lustrous overtones of Josephine Bruce—and with the scent of Mallerin or Papa Meilland. All on one plant with the constitution of Peace!

A pipe-dream of a grey-whiskered veteran pottering in his garden of a summer evening? Perhaps. But I think it will comè true. There *will* be such a rose. And, in all probability, before the 1970s are out. I am reminded of a remark made by old Kordes, not so long ago: 'It is just as well no rose is perfect, for then we would have nothing to strive for.'

Kordes has a winner, among its kind, in his heavily-scented bright turkey-red Ernest H. Morse. Alec Cocker of Aberdeen, gets near with his 1970 introduction Alec's Red. But still the real target has not been hit: the dark, glowing crimson so near to men's, if not women's hearts. And in these days of plant copyright protection, there could be £1,000,000 or more in royalties for anyone likely to hit it. The jackpot red, if ever there was one.

Come to think, Jackpot wouldn't be a bad name for such a new-comer, for, with the inevitable concentrating of breeding lines, it is almost certain to be a descendant of old General Jack—Général Jacqueminot, if you insist on his name in full. For this old crimson hybrid perpetual, raised as long ago as 1853, is now virtually the daddy of all our modern dark red hybrid teas—even though he hadn't such a really deep colour himself. According to researches made in America as far back as 1944, no fewer than 530 named roses were listed then as being descendants of old Jack. Today, through the dominating influence of Crimson Glory, one of his ultimate progeny, there must be 1,000 'Jacqueminots' in known cultivation past or present. The odds are all in favour of our Jack-pot of the 1970s being another of the line. But I am equally sure of this. Whatever combinations of mathematics and mechanics are employed to engineer his coming, Jackpot's birth-story won't be half so romantic as that of his ancient forbear.

Général Jacqueminot—General Jack to florists the world over—is one of those roses whose ancestry is almost lost in the mists of time. So much of his background and breeding is officially listed now in such half-doubting terms as 'probably' and 'believed'. Per-haps they are mere verbal bolt-holes for the scientific purists; those who must see everything in clear black or white. What is accepted, unchallenged, is that Général Jacqueminot was a chance seedling: a child of the open air, raised from an outdoor pollination made in his garden at Montpelier in the mid-1800s by a French amateur raiser of high aims but unscientific practices, one Monsieur Roussel. It is listed as being 'probably a seedling' of the old semi-double China rose, Gloire des Rosomanes, itself brought out in 1825.

Old General Jack—as Jackpot will never be—was given away. Monsieur Roussel died before he could market it and left it in his will to his gardener, one Rousselet. Monsieur Rousselet took it with him to Paris and called it Général Jacqueminot after one of Napoleon's commanders at Waterloo, a cavalryman who broke his own sword rather than disarm his soldiers.

Général Jacqueminot, long-stemmed, twenty-six petals, clear

red, but with a scent which everyone said was out of this world, came on to the market in 1853; stayed in the Rose Society's select lists for fifty-three years; and is still under propagation in some nurseries today. I know of two old plants of it in a friend's garden, each now more than sixty years old, nearly five feet tall and bearing their offerings of heavenly-scented blooms en masse every summer. Since its first introduction at least five attempts have been made to boost its sales by re-introductions under different names. Yes, old General Jack was, is, as good as that. The new boy, Jackpot, will certainly have something to live up to . . . and beat.

Yellow Roses

It came with a great flourish of trumpets. Nothing like the elaborate glossy catalogues on which some nurserymen today spend up to £50,000 or more to advertise their wares, but at least with the biggest-ever publicity boost in the horticultural press of the time. For this was the masterpiece, the rose every gardener in the world would want for his own. It was called Rayon d'Or and growers in England and France spent thousands of pounds, millions of francs, stocking up with this, the first yellow hybrid tea rose. It would set the seal on Joseph Pernet-Ducher's many achievements, they said. It was history-making. Well, so Rayon d'Or was. But it was also a flop. It just wouldn't grow.

Plants succumbed to die-back like the plague. Nurseries on both sides of the English Channel had their entire stocks wiped out, long before any of them could get a single plant of the newcomer off to their customers. Rayon d'Or was in the record books, and in the catalogues, right enough. But it was the rose that hardly got off the ground!

It seems strange, looking back now, that yellow hybrid teas were unknown when I was a boy. Indeed, it is even harder to realise that in 1884, just fourteen years before I was born, the famous Cheshunt firm of William Paul, so often called the father of the English rose, listed in his catalogue only nine hybrid teas all told as against 800-odd hybrid perpetuals. And there was no yellow flower among the hybrid perpetuals at all.

The parents of Rayon d'Or were Mme Mélanie Soupert, a creamy pink flushed hybrid tea—not unlike a slimmer La Jolla, if I remember aright—crossed with Soleil d'Or, a carmine flushed orange-gold rose, officially listed as a hybrid *foetida*. Soleil d'Or had been originated by crossing the old deep red hybrid perpetual Antoine Ducher with the species *foetida*, the Austrian rose.

Pernet-Ducher had been experimenting with such a cross for years, and there alone is a story of patience, so typical of the whole business of rose-breeding, especially in the old rule of thumb, instinct-guided days. Scant success rewarded his efforts—for the reason, as we now know but which old Joseph had no means of telling—that the two intended parents were of different genetical make-up. But, just as he was about to abandon the attempt, after some fifteen years of trying, the miracle happened and two seedlings resulted. One was a tall-growing single-flowered rose that proved sterile as a breeder and was finally marketed as Rhodophile Graveraux, to enjoy a short life as a pillar rose. The other was an unnamed specimen of typical hybrid perpetual characteristics, except that it showed an unusual plentitude of thorns and bore distinct touches of yellow and orange on its basically pink blooms. It was that one which became the parent of Soleil d'Or. And Soleil inherited the orange and gold but little of the pink. Untidy grower that she may have been, she was to prove prolific enough as a breeder to compensate Pernet-Ducher for all his earlier disappointments as he strove to create his new race of hardy yellows that could bring the missing colour to bedding schemes.

A gardener's nightmare she might have been, but she was the hybridist's dream-girl. For it was Soleil d'Or that founded that race of startling colours, typified by Mme Edouard Herriot, the Daily Mail rose, that became known as pernetianas.

The good Mme Edouard, incidentally, is probably the only rose ever to be referred to by two names at once. The reason for this is typically Gallic. When the London *Daily Mail* in 1913 offered a prize of £1,000 for the best rose submitted to an international panel of judges, the stipulation was that the winner should be called Daily Mail. Now M. Ducher submitted his new eye-catching flame beauty, obtained from a Soleil d'Or and Caroline Testout union, and won. But he had a confession to make, he said, before he could accept the £1,000 prize. In fact, he was in some predicament. For he had already promised to name this beauty in honour of Madame Edouard Herriot, wife of the worthy mayor of Lyons—the town-councillor who was in time to become President of France. What could the *Daily Mail* do, in all the circumstances, but to agree to the bi-lingual compromise?

The pernetianas, for all their brightness and startling new colours, were characteristically reluctant growers, susceptible to die-back, ready victims of black spot. But two of the more reliable performers were yellows, Mrs George Beckwith, produced in 1922, and Souvenir de Claudius Pernet, named after one of Pernet-Ducher's two sons and business partners, both killed in the First World War. Later in the line came an even more impressive yellow, Julien Potin, and this one, I notice, stayed in our own sales list until the second war broke out. It wasn't long after that that the pernetianas as a class were involved in what I can only call the first merger in the rose-business—perhaps take-over would be the better, more up-to-date word. For their breeding got so involved with the 'straight bred' hybrid teas, that the rose societies of the world finally decided that the two classes should henceforth be united as one, simply to be known as hybrid teas.

Yellow roses, over the years, have given me infinite pleasure. Mrs Beatty, a B. R. Cant creation in that soft lemon-primrose shade of old Maréchal Niel, is now seldom seen, but was a never-failing delight in her day. McGredy's Yellow, which followed her in similar colouring, is now ageing too. Unhappily, nothing in quite the same subtle softness of hue has yet come to replace them.

Phyllis Gold, a bright yellow hybrid tea and one of Julien Potin's descendants raised by the distinguished English hybridist Herbert Robinson of Burbage, was one of the earliest roses to bear the label 'A Wheatcroft Introduction'. I staged it to win a gold medal at the National Rose Society summer show in 1934, alongside the same raiser's dark crimson Christopher Stone.

Kordes used another of our gold medal winning, Robinson-produced introductions, Walter Bentley—of Mrs Sam McGredy lineage—crossed with Condesa de Sastago, to give us Golden Sun.

This, on its arrival in 1957, made every lover of the deep golden yellow pay immediate homage. It was a perfect shape; had a depth of colour hitherto unknown, and a liveliness in its flower that made it an instant show sensation. The liveliness, unfortunately, did not extend to the plant. Like Mabel Morse, a McGredy introduction in the same colour range thirty-five years before, Golden Sun reserves its best performances for its maiden year. There is marked and rapid deterioration in plant virility after that. It is still in some demand today by exhibitors willing to raise their own stocks of maidens each year. And by breeders, in Europe and America alike, valuing it as a sterling parent of new varieties. But most commercial growers have now dropped it. For it is Golden Sun that, to quote Herb Swim, 'looks a million dollars' growing in the nursery lines but is a very quickly setting sun after that. If you do still grow it, tolerating a spindly plant for the sake of its wonderful blooms, may I offer a tip: with me it always responds best to light pruning.

16 Belle Blonde, a Meilland product, two years younger than Golden Sun, remains one of my favourites as she has been since I first saw her, a fair, golden beauty with the freshness of a country girl. She is bred three-quarters Peace—a product of Peace crossed with Lorraine, which itself was Peace × Mme Mallerin. In no way resembling Peace in stature but with typical Peace sturdiness on a bush a little below average height, she is never out of flower. Whatever the weather I can always cut enough first-class Belle Blondes from our nursery stock to be sure of a compelling display at any exhibition. We had Belle Blonde on trial for three years at Wheatcroft's before we put her into commercial production and were showing her, unnamed, on all the big occasions. One year I presented a bouquet of her golden offerings to a kinswoman of our Queen, Princess Alice, Countess of Athlone, who was celebrating her golden wedding.

Princess Alice, taking a special interest in any new variety, laughingly suggested that when this one was eventually named it should be called Golden Wedding. Unfortunately, this was not possible as an earlier variety bore the same name. When the time came to catalogue our newcomer, in 1955, the name Belle Blonde came to me. I still think it is one of my happiest choices.

Yellows today are a multitude. Every season one, at least, comes forth with the strongest claims for inclusion in every up-to-date nursery list. Of all the newcomers one in particular has captured my heart: Diorama, one of the last creations of that old master, the Dutchman George de Ruiter. This is a Peace × Beauté, not a true self-yellow, for its flowers, in their earliest hours, bear an orange tinge on their wide-flung outer petals. But it is an intriguing beauty, with Beauté's lustrous sheen inherited in abundance. There is a refreshing fragrance, too.

And that reminds me. Do you know why tea roses are so called? The class was developed from roses brought here, and to France, from China. And the story is that someone took a long deep sniff at the first of the new line and said it reminded him of the fragrance exuding from a newly-opened chest of China tea! So tea roses they became . . . for evermore.

Fact or fiction? Who knows? The time was the early 1880s. But this I can add. My wife says our present instant brew doesn't smell a bit like Mrs Herbert Stevens—or *devoniensis*, either!

Willi Kordes

At the time when a teen-aged Harry Wheatcroft was lodged in Wormwood Scrubs jail for holding a strong conscientious objection to war—a conviction for which I still don't apologise—Wilhelm Kordes was languishing on the Isle of Man. His particular crime was to have been born German and to have been resident here, in business as a rose-growing nurseryman, at the time His Britannic Majesty's government declared war on the Kaiser's Germany. Willi, already established, and I, then with no thought of entering the rose business, stayed as governmental guests, unknown to each other, for years. Then, when it was all over, we went our different ways.

Willi was the son of a Hamburg general nurseryman who later turned to specialisation in roses. Willi himself had been apprenticed to the craft as far back as 1905. After spells on rose nurseries in Switzerland and the Cap d'Antibes, France—the Meilland country—he arrived in Britain in 1912 to take a job in the establishment of S. Bide and Sons, one of our oldest firms, near Farnham in Surrey. There he met another German, Max Krause, who was in charge of Bide's greenhouses and propagation operations. Max, a rose man of great experience, had previously worked on nurseries in Dorset and Sussex and with Bees at Chester. Young Willi lodged in Krause's home in Farnham.

'And eventually,' he says, 'this pair of foreigners started their

Willi Kordes.

own rose and general nursery firm of W. Kordes and Krause, at Witley, near Godalming, in Surrey.

'We were doing well, looking happily to the future, until in the first week of September 1914 they asked us, very politely, to pass through a barbed wire fence into a concentration camp for dangerous Germans, near Aldershot.'

From there, it was next stop Isle of Man. And when Willi came out, on February 26th 1919, he found he was to be deported, along with Krause, as an 'undesirable alien', with strict orders not to attempt to return to Britain for at least ten years. The flourishing nursery of Kordes and Krause was confiscated. 'And the crowning blow,' says Willi, 'is that when I visited the nursery years later, the whole place was built over with greenhouses and they were growing carnations there, not roses.'

Willi treats his internment and subsequent deportation with a shrug of his broad shoulders. As just one of those things: the fortunes of a war over which he had no control and, like me, no desire to participate in. His best friends, he says, are still the British. But my great regret is that Willi isn't British too. I think that he and Max might have been—but for the senseless damn-everything-German edicts of the authorities in 1914–18. The same sort of blind stupidity that caused the magnificent white rose Frau Karl Druschki to be renamed Snow Queen in our catalogues—simply because it was German. 'Put this stiff, military-looking rose with no scent and a German name on the scrap heap or send her to Potsdam' wrote a correspondent to the Rose Society *Annual* of 1915. And in the face of such bigoted frenzy, what chance had Willi and Max?

But if they *had* been allowed to remain in Britain, what then? I have no doubt in my own mind that Britain would today have been the leading rose-raising country in the world, instead of also-running in fourth place behind the Americans, the French and the Germans. The Kordes introductions—and there were so many from Willi and his son Reimar—would have turned the scale if they had been bred at Witley, Surrey, within forty miles of London. As well they might!

Now what makes a rose-grower? I'd say patience and determination and an insatiable urge for perfection. And Willi Kordes, that

Josephine Bruce (*photo Downward*)

Papa Meilland,
the rose and
the man

Ernest H. Morse

Belle Blonde

King's Ransom

Diorama

Bed of Pink
Favourite

My Choice

Godfrey Winn

Battle of Britain

With Gene Boerner and Willi Kordes

Harry, Christopher and David Wheatcroft with Mathias Tantau and a new yellow rose from Tantau's, **Sunblest**

'undesirable alien', certainly has all of these, together with an eye for beauty such as few men possess.

Determination? Listen to this from the man who says 'As an apprentice it took me three years on a general nursery to learn the difference between a *sambucus* (elderberry) and a *malus* (crab apple).' I quote from a letter Willi wrote me a few years ago:

'On my deportation from Britain in 1919 I joined my brother Hermann and we started in our present nursery at Sparrieshoop, twenty miles from Hamburg. Max Krause came with us but went off on his own, fifteen miles from here, two years later. The first year we had 40,000 understocks (the briar seedlings on which the cultivars are budded). But times were bad and we sometimes had to sell first-class roses for only a few German schillings a hundred. Then, with the German mark falling all the time, we took the precautions of selling only for foreign currency, so that we could re-sell some of this, if need arose, to keep our men at work and in food and clothes. These were wild times in Germany, with two men out of work to every one in and with the whole country financed by printing on paper.'

Then came Adof Hitler. Says Kordes: 'Hatred of anything foreign, or anything with foreign connections, was at the bottom of his gaining absolute control of Germany, including the trade in roses. Any money we earned from export now had to be delivered within forty-eight hours to the state bank—no more financing our own business, as we had done in the years between 1919 and 1923.'

By 1928 the Kordes firm had reached a milestone in their career, with a million plants sold. By 1933, under Hitler, production had dropped to a mere third of this total and prices were again falling. Once more, Willi and his brother met the challenge.

'By 1935,' he writes, 'we had recovered and when Adolf went mad in 1939 we had 1,500,000 plants on our fields and under growing contracts.'

But by then Willi and I had met. He had raised and introduced his first world-wide hit, Crimson Glory. And around the same time, Wheatcrofts were launching a glowing dark scarlet scented rose, Christopher Stone, raised by that doyen of British breeders, Herbert Robinson. Willi recalls our first meeting: 'It must have been 1936 or 1937, at one of your English shows. I was looking at the Crimson Glory shown by my friend Ernest Morse, of Brundall,

D

near Norwich. Nearby a very hairy specimen of *homo sapiens* was arranging a stand with Christopher Stone.'

That, of course, was me. We were introduced and chatted about the two varieties. Kordes resumed our argument on their respective merits some years later, saying 'Well, both have their place. But I'm sure if anybody could make Christopher Stone grow as big a plant as Crimson Glory it would still be selling in quantity. I tried, but had no success.'

Even though it has now lost a lot of its inborn vitality and is to-day perhaps little more than a museum piece, Crimson Glory deservedly managed to keep a place at the top of the sales lists for more than thirty years. Christopher Stone is still available but had nothing like Crimson Glory's run of popularity.

The war, I believe, could be blamed for upsetting unlucky Christopher's career. But it wasn't the only rose to suffer. And the second war didn't spare rose-growers either. For look what happened to Willi and me the second time our countries went to war. Our Wheatcroft fields, then at Ruddington, just outside Nottingham, had to be ploughed up to make way for wheat, sugar beet and potatoes. The greenhouses in which we had forced our early show roses were turned over to tomatoes. Four hundred-thousand rose trees, all in full bloom, and four hundred-thousand thriving briars, already budded for sale the next year, had to be bulldozed out and burned. My brother Alfred and I managed to save a few —no more than six of each—of our best varieties and these we replanted in the back gardens of our homes. Neither of us could bear to be around to see the funeral pyres of the roses to which we had dedicated ourselves.

Later we learned that we need not have ploughed our precious plants up at all. We could have kept the lot. But orders then had a curious way of becoming variously interpreted.

When it came to re-starting after the war, we had the budding eyes from about a couple of hundred trees, growing in our gardens. But no understocks! The briars on to which British nurserymen budded their cultivated varieties had largely been imported— mainly from Holland—now this source was lost to us. What to do? Alfred and I put our heads together and decided that if the Ministry of Food was marketing rose hip syrup, they must somewhere have the seeds of the hips available after the syrup had been extracted. We wrote to them and found that we could indeed buy these seeds. They were there in the sludge, at the factories. So we bought gallons of these sticky dregs; dried out the seeds and sowed them. And a fine crop of briars resulted. They were a little uneven compared with present day commercial standards but at least we were on our feet again.

But what about Kordes? His troubles, it seemed, were only just beginning. He had all the glass in his greenhouses broken during the British air raids on nearby Hamburg and a few plants in the fields destroyed too.

'In the spring of 1945,' he says, 'we had a field of roses numbering some 2,500 plants. And we had 15,000 briars, of all possible sorts and thicknesses. We had to hide them behind walls or conceal small plantations in the middle of rye-fields, because food had become more precious than gold or diamonds.'

Then the gardener's oldest enemy, hard-killing frost, took a hand and hit Kordes harder, even, than the war. 'Of those 15,000 briars,' he recalls, 'all but 1,500 were killed by frost. The game seemed over.' But Kordes, always the eternal optimist, began yet again, still with his briars hidden from prying eyes behind walls and hedges. From friends and old customers growing roses for cut flowers he managed to obtain a few hundred buds of some 100 varieties—many of them unsuited for general garden purposes. Yet once more a cruel winter was to beat him. 'We lost all the plants of the varieties we were testing for future development and ninety-nine per cent of the budded understock never greened out in the spring. We did manage to save a few seedlings but there was a full year's loss of germination in the greenhouses. The seed had become so frozen that germination did not take place until a year later,' he recalls.

Once more, it looked as if the Kordes empire was reaching its end. But still Willi kept going. And today, looking back on his post-war gloom, Willi can say that out of it emerged a bonus triumph. For it was in these years, when almost everything around them was blackened to the roots, that Willi's *kordesii* climbers emerged still green and smiling.

These were the varieties Willi had worked on, crossing selected hybrid teas with such species as *Rosa spinosissima*, the Scotch or burnet rose, to develop climbers hardy enough to withstand the severe north German winters. Today they are in rose gardens all over the world, smiling through the snow and frosts. And he discovered, by a chance seedling, that they would also flower repeatedly through the summer. Until The New Dawn had arrived in 1930 as a freak—a sport from the once-a-year flowering wichuriana rambler Dr W. Van Fleet and destined to become the first rose in the world ever patented—none of our climbers was truly remontant, or repeat flowering. But these *kordesii* hybrids were. And they were beauties, like Maigold, Dortmund, Kassel, Hamburger Phoenix, Frühlingsgold and Frühlingsmorgen, a complete new range that was to change all our ideas about the uses and limitations of climbing varieties.

No one has contributed more lasting beauty to our gardens than Willi Kordes. No one has more deserved his success. Today the yearly output of his nurseries is 3,000,000 plants, with 1,000,000 of that total going into the gardens of private customers in Germany, 500,000 being shipped for export and the rest sold to wholesale or forcing houses on the Continent. The independence and courage of the man is, I think, summed up in a footnote he wrote in that letter to me:

'The stage was really set for our new battle for roses in 1945, when my son Reimar got back from the war with no greater handicap than a stiff right arm, and my brother Hermann's three boys —all in Russia from the beginning—returned to us with only one lost leg between them. We knew then that we could, were meant to, go ahead.'

So next time you see the chiselled majesty of Perfecta or watch the bees dancing lightly over the drifting snow-mass of Iceberg (finally introduced by Willi's son), spare a thought for the trials and tribulations of the ever-courageous, ever-courteous, ever-smiling man who gave them all to us.

57

Climbers and Ramblers

Round the world in the service of the rose, I have seen many wonders. Hybrid teas like Mrs Sam McGredy, never more than three feet tall at home, growing to towering giants of near nine foot stature in the United States, particularly in California and at Portland, Oregon. A bush of Frensham, the floribunda, seven feet across and every inch as tall, flourishing in Bermuda. Roses as far as the eye could see, a vast ocean of colour, stretching across 1,500 acres on the then headquarters of the Jackson and Perkins 'empire' at Newark, New Jersey. The freshness of New Zealand's roses; the delights, all too seldom seen at home, of the 'hot weather varieties' revelling in the Australian sun. All these will live for ever in my memory. But in trying to decide where I have seen the finest roses, the most beautiful individual blooms, I can arrive at no other answer than in Britain. And I would certainly name two of our professional gardens where the rose is exclusive mistress, as the finest of their kind in the world. They are Queen Mary's rose gar- 31, 32, den in London's Regent's Park, and the National Rose Society's 33, 34 garden and trial ground at St. Albans.

On the Continent, there is nothing, in my opinion, to beat the magnificent gardens at Lyons in France and at Madrid, the national home of the rose in Spain. I have for years been a member of the international panel, judging the new varieties there, and on each

Looking down on the Madrid rose gardens.

The showground of the Jackson and Perkins 'empire'.

visit to Madrid I have found new wonders, new delights. Built against the backdrop of a towering, tree-covered hillside, on a site that was once a municipal rubbish dump, this garden impresses first by its very situation—almost in the heart of the bustling capital city.

So many Spanish-raised roses fail to show their natural beauty in our colder climate. I have had many on trial, yet, to my great disappointment, have been able to recommend comparatively few as likely to succeed in your gardens, under average British conditions. That is no criticism of the Spanish raisers. A lot of our own introductions won't respond abroad, in sun-baked gardens where their fewer petals, by Continental standards, open too quickly. In Madrid, Spanish roses are at home and their response is sheer beauty. But my lasting memory of Madrid will always be—as doubtless it will for many another Englishman—the sight of its magnificent specimens of climbing Peace, stretching to the heavens, completely enveloping open pergolas nine feet high and twelve feet across. And each carrying its burden of a massive crop of perfect blooms.

Now why should this riot of Peace particularly impress Englishmen? We've got climbing Peace in this country and have had for years. It sported with Lee Brady, at Tyler in Texas, in 1950 and with Kordes in Germany a year later. From both sources there has been plenty of budding material. So it's not the novelty of climbing Peace so far as we are concerned, it's just the novelty of seeing climbing Peace in bloom. For this is one of the really few failings Meilland's great rose has ever had. It will reward us in Britain with all its beauty in its dwarf form, even as a standard. Yet, as a climber, whether it has been Brady's stock or Kordes's, it has been shy and stubborn to produce its loveliness. But only with us! Everywhere else, it seems, climbing Peace is one of the unquestionable greats.

In a few places, mostly in America, I believe, it is recorded as being slow to establish itself after transplantation from its nursery bed. But once it has got a foothold, away it goes, even there, like an unrestrained giant. Not with us! Budding wood from several confirmed free-blooming sources has been introduced into this country from time to time, in the hope of getting climbing Peace's performance to equal its efforts abroad. But it's still no go—or rather, plenty of 'go' but precious few blooms. Many of my fellow nursery-men have, like myself, now got fed up with trying and have dropped climbing Peace from our lists. And no one can say we're particu-larly eager to drop rewarding climbers! I have just been checking through the latest catalogue of Harry Wheatcroft and Sons against the last one produced before the war, (I mean Hitler's war of course) for the then firm of Wheatcroft Brothers. A time-gap of thirty years or so, perhaps the most rewarding thirty years in the rose's history. Only three varieties remain on our current list from those we cherished before Hitler so rudely interrupted, and all three are climbers: The New Dawn, so prophetically-named; the elegant Mermaid; and the ever-enthusiastic Albertine, ready to spread her shining green leaves and nostalgically scented copper apricot flowers over every obstacle in sight.

Except for Albertine, the day of the once-blooming climbers, like that of the ramblers (Dorothy Perkins) and the *wichuraianas* (American Pillar) is done. Not for the time-pressed amateur gar-eners of the 1970s that long, laborious chore of annual pruning (each tree a forest of stems and thorns), tieing in new wood as it grows, spraying, cosseting, just for two week's display a year. No, it's only the so-called perpetual flowering climbers—New Dawn, Danse du Feu, Golden Showers, Hamburger Phoenix, Joseph's Coat, and their like, that are readily saleable now.

In his efforts to produce perpetual flowering—technically de-scribed as remontant—climbers, the rose breeder is struggling all the time against nature. For the hereditary instinct of all climbers, except the hybrid tea sports—and some of these can be shy with their second crop—is to produce a mass of flowers just once a year. Perpetual flowering is what is known as a recessive characteristic.

Surprisingly to me, for so much advance has been made in this section, only one of the modern so-called large-flowered climbers has yet been awarded the Rose Society's gold medal: the yellow, delightfully rewarding Casino, raised by the present Sam McGredy, fourth of that ilk. I say surprisingly because, when for the first time in its history the Society awarded a gold medal to anything but an outright exhibition rose, it was to a climber, but nothing like such a beauty as Casino. The year was 1883, just ten years after gold medals for roses were first awarded, and the variety was Turner's Crimson Rambler. It was as big a break, in its way, as was The

New Dawn in our time. And the advent of Mr Turner's winner was a story in itself.

It didn't make its public début until after a royal visit of inspection and approval. Word reached Queen Victoria—a devoted rose admirer so it is said—of an unusual new variety growing in a nursery at Slough, not far from her beloved Windsor. She made up her mind that she must see it. And in Charles Turner's garden she saw his Crimson Rambler.

Now Turner was already something of a name in the horticultural world. He had already introduced the famous Mrs Sinkins pink and Cox's Orange Pippin apple. When he sent Turner's Crimson Rambler to the National Rose Society's summer show at the old Crystal Palace not long after Queen Victoria had seen and commended it, it won an immediate gold medal. And its impact on the public must have been as great as it had been on the judges. Within weeks of the show, Turner is reputed to have said that he had taken orders for 9,000 plants of the variety, at the then princely price of half a guinea a time. Mr Turner, not unnaturally, was not slow to speak of the success of his new variety but of its origins he professed to know little. Except that it was of the multiflora group and had been brought to this country from Japan, at the request of a retired Scots businessman, then living near Edinburgh.

More detailed investigations showed that it had, in fact, first been found growing in a garden in Tokyo, by a Scot, one Robert Smith, who was then, in 1873, professor of engineering at Tokyo University. He had sent a specimen of it home to his friend Robert Jenner at Edinburgh who, for want of a better title, had christened it The Engineer's Rose. And, as The Engineer's Rose, it had apparently already attained considerable local popularity in and around the Scottish capital before it came into Turner's possession. In fact, a small local nurseryman, John Gilbert, is now believed to have brought it into commercial propagation in 1885, six years before Queen Victoria heard of it.

Turner, as shrewd a businessman as they come, bought up Gilbert's entire stock, so it is said, after seeing the variety on a visit north. So The Engineer's Rose became Turner's Crimson Rambler and the astute Mr Turner obtained considerable orders from it from growers in the United States. In salesmanship, old Charles was way ahead of his time, he might even have been able to teach me something! But if he had hoped that this variety would perpetuate his name, he was to be disappointed. The 'Turner' tag was soon dropped and the variety became known simply as Crimson Rambler.

Yet there was, it seems, an even older name in existence for it before Jenner christened it The Engineer's Rose. For it had first been shown to our old friend Robert Smith, apparently, when it was growing in the garden of a certain Tokyo house of entertainment, where the resident ladies had called it The Ten Sisters—no doubt after ten memorable girls of their kind. A visiting British sailor had found it there and introduced it to Smith. So, from a Tokyo brothel to a royal garden in England, Crimson Rambler certainly moved a long way. And it was to create a considerable influence on our roses for a long time. Nearly 400 crossings to produce new multiflora climbers were made from it.

It also became the progenitor, through its daughter Tausendschön, of two dwarf sports. And these, according to many experts, eventually gave rise to the polyantha pom-pom family—such as the Orleans Rose, Mrs W. H. Cutbush, Cameo and Coral Cluster —which are really the ancestors of the vast assembly of beauties we know today as floribundas. And Crimson Rambler, in my opinion at least, may well have led us into that other new field that is of engrossing interest today: blue roses.

Blue Roses

Far be it from me to disturb the ladies of the flower arranging guilds. They have done much to bring a love and knowledge of flowers to a vast army of enthusiastic housewives who might otherwise have been content with a single aspidistra in a glazed pot or an overdrawn geranium struggling for existence on the kitchen window sill. Yet I cannot fail to raise a bushy eyebrow at one consequence of their pursuits. Just how many freak plants, I wonder, have my fellow nurserymen, not merely the rose-specialists, been led to bring into unworthy existence merely to pander to the flower-arrangers' taste for the bizarre?

In our own field, we have had brown-coloured roses, tan-coloured roses, olive-tinged roses, even roses that looked like dirty washing before any of those 'brighter than bright' aids were marketed. Many of these so-called novelties, I am sure, would have been ruthlessly uprooted at the seedling stage in grandfather's day, discarded as being the inevitable, unwanted, ugly sisters in a family of beauties. But if we blame the flower-arrangers for this, it is only right to pose another question. How far have these same good ladies been responsible for pushing us in our quest for the blue rose? My guess at the answer is: a mightly long way, and every credit to them for it. If it hadn't been for their enthusiasm, I'm convinced that blue roses would have stayed forgotten. For the search for the true blue in the species *Rosa* had been abandoned as an impossible dream, another El Dorado, for almost seventy years. Until, just after the Second World War, the flower-arrangers brought our thoughts back on to the track.

The first step towards revival was inauspicious enough. The present Sam McGredy's father had produced, just before the war, a seedling obtained by crossing the progeny of two reds, Southport and Sir David Davies, with that of another anonymous seedling from the creamy white Mrs Charles Lamplough, a daughter of marble-white Frau Karl Druschki. It flowered a muzzy grey, a colour undistinguished enough for the newcomer to be referred to by the forthright gardeners at Portadown as 'The Mouse'. And old Sam McGredy himself was so little impressed that he didn't attempt commercial production. Instead, he sent the rose to the United States into the custody of the late Gene Boerner.

Now Gene, as discerning as they come, saw far more in this Irish immigrant than any mere sales possibilities. In fact he was so enthusiastic he called it 'the first major break of our time'. And, in the hunt for the blue, so it was to prove. The name Grey Pearl was given to the newcomer. According to accounts, it was suggested by the celebrated opera singer Helen Jepson while she was visiting the nurseries of Jackson and Perkins, with which Boerner was associated. Miss Jepson was asked what she thought of the Irish newcomer and said: 'Oh, it's like the colour of my grey pearls.' So Grey Pearl it became.

It went into commerce across the Atlantic in 1945 but not until 1950 did it come back for production here. Constance Spry, a year after its return, referred to it as 'nun-like' and went on to extol 'its subtle, muted beauty, even though it has been received with disparagement by the critics.' Grey Pearl, in fact, proved to be rather a turncoat. It *could* look lavender grey. It could equally look pale tan or weak olive green or even a horrid brown, according to the weather. With its short centre petals and its tendency to winter die-back, it was inevitably quickly doomed as a garden plant, as Sam McGredy had feared. But for Gene Boerner, the idea was there. This one 'had something'. And Grey Pearl was to herald the re-birth of the blues.

Boerner used Grey Pearl crossed with Pinocchio to create Lavender Pinocchio. One American lady described this as a 'very sad rose'. But it was the first blue break into the floribunda class as we know it today. Gene used his Pearl again to give us Lavender Garnette in 1958 and by a Lavender Pinocchio cross the next year he gave us yet another floribunda, Lavender Princess, in the new colour range. And he went on, using the same blood lines, to give us further advances.

But back to the hybrid teas. Three years after Grey Pearl's European debut, Carlos Camrubi, a Spanish grower operating within the consortium Universal Rose Selection (I was one of the founder members), introduced the grey-mauve Tristesse. This was a cross between the flame-coloured Charles P. Kilham, one of the ancestors of Peace, and the two-toned pink Betty Uprichard. It had a more stable colour than Grey Pearl but the same short petals. And it went the same way.

Next came Prélude, a Meilland introduction, of far better shape —more like a thin Ophelia—and again with Charles P. Kilham blood in its pedigree. 'A useful rose for the decorator' was one description of it. But although it sold well with us as a novelty, few gardeners seemed to share the arrangers' enthusiasm for it. The truth is that few of these early 'blues' were anything but a pale shade of lilac-grey and with their poor weather-resistance were of little use in bedding. But Meilland still insisted to me that Prélude would really be the start of something—that was why he had called it Prélude. And so it was to prove.

McGredy brought out Lilac Time, tracing back, through Luis Brinas, to Ophelia, but this one outdoors was often more pink than lilac, a criticism that could also be applied to the later variety, Lilac Rose, brought out by Sanday's of Bristol. Lavender Queen, introduced in America by Frank Raffel, showed the same tendency towards pink as its dominant colour.

Sterling Silver, a Peace seedling and an American (Jackson and Perkins) introduction of 1957, went into my garden and perhaps into yours, too. For this one was truly the best at the time. But it failed to inherit Peace's robustness and when it, too, came to suffer its douchings under what we called the English summer, most people soon lost interest.

Edward Le Grice, from his prolific nursery near North Walsham in Norfolk, gave us the floribunda Lavender Lady by using

Boerner's Lavender Pinocchio, while Meilland broke into the floribunda section in 1958 with his Lavender Girl, again using Charles P. Kilham blood. All these were, in retrospect, steps along the road. It was not until the 1960s that the real advance began to show itself.

Georges Delbard, the French raiser, perhaps found an apt name for this modern rhapsody of the blues when he called his 1961 introduction Waltz Time, even though he marketed it in France as Saint Exupéry. Heure Mauve, a Mallerin variety (Prélude crossed with a Caroline Testout rose, Simone) came to challenge Delbard's introduction a year later.

24 Le Grice brought out his delightful little floribunda Lilac Charm but only seldom could it produce, out of doors, the same startling brilliance of red-tipped stamens against soft mauve petals that it shows under glass. Boerner gave us Lavender Charm, using Sterling Silver as a parent, and then came Lens's Blue Diamond and Simon Dot's Intermezzo, which carried both Grey Pearl and Prélude blood—'the best of both worlds', as one breeder put it at the time. But Pedro Dot, Simon's octogenarian father, scored over his son when, in 1968, he brought out the high-centred, richly scented

19 and, for a blue, comparatively strong-growing Godfrey Winn. This, with Tantau's Blue Moon (in spite of colour instability on its

25 outer petals) and Kordes's Cologne Carnival, look at the time of writing, to be the best blues yet.

Will we ever produce a rose with a really true delphinium shade of blue? Your guess is as good as mine. The scientists tell us that although the essential blue pigment, delphinidin, is absent from the rose in its wild state, it could appear in one of our cultivars by a freak of nature called mutation. After all, as they so rightly point out, there is nothing in any rose species resembling the colour of such blooms as Independence, Anna Wheatcroft and Super Star. Yet look how far we've come along *that* 'unnatural' colour line!

So the true-blue rose could still appear. Some day, in your garden you may yet look upon the marvel of a scented hybrid tea, vying in hue with the forget-me-nots underfoot. Until then, 'blues', in my opinion, are unlikely to make any great impact as bedders. But the possibility of just such a breakthrough is exciting enough to have breeders all over the world engaged in the hunt—and spending thousands of pounds, dollars, francs and marks in the process.

Now I wonder if I might offer them a clue, on a possible breeding line no one yet seems to have attempted. I would refer them to Turner's Crimson Rambler, The Engineer's Rose, about which I wrote in my last chapter. For this long-distance traveller produced Veilchenbläu (see my Introduction), an old rambler that came out in 1909 and is still flourishing in some gardens. And Veilchenbläu is still the bluest blue I have ever seen among the roses. Its flowers, especially in the first few hours of morning when the new buds are awakening, really do look like a spilt pot of violet ink. It has also produced a truly amethyst-coloured sport, christened Rose Marie Viaud in France where it originated, but marketed here and in America under the deserved title of Amethyst.

So I'm wondering if some of our present-day hybridists wouldn't make a step forward if they went back to old Veilchenbläu in their breeding lines. Crossed with, perhaps, The New Dawn, it might stand as good a chance as any of yielding a really blue, large-flowered new climber. And from that could surely be bred a bush variety carrying the blue tint that still seems just above the horizon. One other point tends to support my theory. According to many experts, Vielchenbläu has already produced a dwarf sport. Baby Faurax, a deep violet polyantha pom-pom, made its appearance in the early 1920s. Its ancestry was described as 'unknown'. But now all the evidence of microscopic plant cell tests seems to suggest that it was, in fact, a Veilchenbläu 'pup'.

Heredity

Roses, as I've told you, come as strongly under the influence of certain dominating families as do racehorses. Dominant sires, they call them in the places where the thoroughbred is king. And in the realms where the rose is queen, a few outstanding breeding performers are proving just as effective as Hyperion or Solario, even though their role in perpetuating the line may have been as sires (pollen parents·in our language) or dams (seed parents). Any reference book will show how Peace and Crimson Glory, for instance, have influenced many of our latter-day beauties. These two have been the rose breeder's Hyperions of the mid-twentieth century and for thirty years there has been nothing to touch them.

There is scarcely a red rose in modern catalogues that does not carry Crimson Glory blood. And not reds exclusively either. Fashion, that delightful apricot-salmon floribunda with a built-in luminescence that makes it look as if it is laughing back at the sun, is a Crimson Glory seedling. And so, down the generations, is Elizabeth of Glamis, the Fashion of the late 1960s and 1970s.

Peace, as a parent, has been no less prolific. The characteristics, fads and foibles of these elegant ladies have been passed on to their daughters, grand-daughters, even to the third and fourth generations. So, too, have some of their minor failings.

Ena Harkness and her 'brother' crimsons, William Harvey and Red Ensign—all were evolved by amateur Albert Norman from

Maigold and
Dyna Wheatcroft

Casino 21

Danse du Feu

Mermaid (*photo Downward*)

Albertine (*photo Downward*)

Lilac Charm

Blue Moon

Cologne Carnival

Lady Mary Fitzwilliam
(*photos Graham Thomas*)

Chicago Peace

Candy Stripe

Pink Peace

the same Crimson Glory × Southport cross—cannot be blamed for their weak necks, any more than Josephine Bruce or Papa Meilland can for their seeming affection for mildew. All were built-in traits from dear old Crimson Glory and, further back, from the species *Rosa damascena*, the source of their perfume. All the children of *damascena*—if they inherit the scent—also inherit the apparently inseparable handicap of a weak flower stem.

Peace, for her part, is a trifle slow to mature from bud to full bloom, sometimes throws completely 'blind' or flowerless shoots as her first efforts in any season, and visibly resents it if you try to prune her too hard. But so do Eden Rose, Opera, Prima Ballerina, Karl Herbst, Marigold, New Style, all her descendants.

But it is neither Peace nor Crimson Glory, great though they are, which is uppermost in my mind as I write this chapter of thanks to the dominating genealogies of the family *Rosa*. I don't wear a hat —the only one I ever bought (when I was courting) got left on a train—but if I did I would raise it in silent homage to two great performers of even earlier ages—Mme Caroline Testout and her mother Lady Mary Fitzwilliam. For between them they have virtually laid the foundations of every modern rose garden from Nottingham to Nebraska and back, via New Zealand. And on each of them hangs a tale worth telling.

Let me begin with that old charmer, Caroline. For this was the first rose I ever planted: a bush in my mother's garden, at the age of fifteen, when I was a junior clerk in a Nottingham lace factory, long before rose-growing for a living had even crossed my mind. Caroline Testout, full, glowing pink—cabbagey, you'd call it if you have admiring eyes only for such high-pointed centred roses as Ophelia or Summer Sunshine—came into the world even before I did. It was raised in 1890, by the Frenchman Pernet-Ducher, the man who was later to give his name to a whole distinctive rose class, the pernetianas, now merged into the hybrid teas.

Caroline Testout was named after one Madame Caroline Testout, a creator of Victorian fashions, a nineteenth-century Dior who had salons in both London and Paris. It was the best advertisement she ever had, for Caroline the rose has lasted longer in the rose world than any of Madame Testout's creations in the world of fashion. In her climbing form, this rose is still a good seller and

E

rightly so, for there are few more rewarding performers among the climbing hybrid teas. Plant climbing Caroline and you can still be sure of a show!

For sixty years, at least, she was a 'must' with most commercial growers in her bush form when they came to consider their annual budding schedules and the public demand was always there to consume the supply. Only from the 1950s on, in face of the ever-growing tide of post-war varieties, did the grand old lady have to yield her ground. But still her influence is felt. At a rough count, only the other day, I was able to list no fewer than 150 of our modern beauties, most of them still available in some nurseryman's catalogue, whose existence can be traced back to my old darling Caroline.

The old girl was tough—and long-lasting. In Kew Gardens there used to be a bed of Caroline, some 100 plants or so, growing on their own roots, which means they were struck from cuttings, and records show them to have been approaching seventy years old. Another bed of budded Carolines in the same gardens was nearly a half-century in age when both beds were grassed-down in a re-landscaping project two years ago. None of the roses, even then, showed the slightest sign of advancing years. Just try to figure how many 'new' roses must have come and gone in that time!

But Caroline's record as a breeder must, of course, be passed back to her parent, Lady Mary Fitzwilliam, a heavily-scented (unlike Caroline) pink hybrid tea, brought out by a farmer turned rose breeder, Henry Bennett, in 1882. The parents of this one were *Devoniensis*, an old tea rose, crossed with the hybrid perpetual Victor Verdier—an alliance which made Lady Mary a first-generation hybrid tea. And Lady Mary was to prove a pioneer and an aristocrat indeed; the progenitor of all the greatest red roses of our time. As a parent, she is still in demand today by our hybridists, nearly ninety years after her introduction. And thereon hangs another tale, the tale of an aristocrat who, like many another, was almost eliminated in a revolution, or at least condemned to a premature death. For this is the story of Lady Mary Fitzwilliam, a romance with all the flavour of a Scarlet Pimpernel.

After being used by Bennett in several crosses, and by Pernet-Ducher to produce our worthy Caroline, Lady Mary Fitzwilliam

26

The bed at Kew Gardens of seventy-year-old Caroline Testout.

was allowed to fall into a decline. In my own copy of that classic manual *The Book of the Rose* by the Reverend Andrew Foster-Melliar, there appear these fateful words against Lady Mary's name: 'Eliminated from this edition' (the third edition dated 1910). It could have been no consolation to her and her devotees to find the same damning verdict recorded against her parent, Victor Verdier. The rose world, it seemed, had no further use for Lady Mary. But enter now her Scarlet Pimpernel who was to snatch her from utter extinction: our old friend Willi Kordes.

'Caroline Testout was always a great favourite of mine,' Willi wrote to me. 'But I wanted a scented Caroline, so I tried to pollinate her with Général Jacqueminot (the old deeply scented, dark red, hybrid perpetual). But none of these seedlings showed as I'd hoped.'

So Kordes tried again and this time crossed a Caroline descendant, Superb with the American-bred Crimson Sensation, itself of Caroline blood. Lady Mary lineage occurred four times in that pedigree. The result was Cathrine Kordes, virtually a crimson Testout but, like Caroline, still lacking that elusive quality, scent. Once more Kordes tried, this time crossing Cathrine with the English rose, W. E. Chaplin. And their progeny came dark red and scented. Scented so strongly that when you entered a room it could be almost overpowering. It was named Crimson Glory and, as I've told you, a real glory it has been.

But what happened to Lady Mary Fitzwilliam while all this was going on? Kordes, now at the peak of his triumph, made a careful check on all his breeding records and decided that the one rose that had given him scent was Lady Mary Fitzwilliam. He decided to use her again. And to do so he had to have her growing in his own trial grounds. The decision was far easier reached than the achievement. Eventually, after prolonged searching, he was able to obtain some bud-wood of Lady Mary from the German national rose garden and trial ground at Sangerhausen. Lady Mary's future seemed restored. But another of those desperately hard German winters wiped out Kordes's entire stock of Lady Mary Fitzwilliam. And not only his but also that of his only known source of further supply, the 'old rose' beds at Sangerhausen. In desperation Willi tried throughout Germany to find a surviving Lady Mary specimen—just one. No luck. And no luck, again, when he advertised his need in the rose journals of the world.

When his final appeal to British growers in the Rose Society's Annual brought no response, Willi told me: 'I am convinced Lady Mary Fitzwilliam has now completely gone out of existence. No more in the world. What a loss!'

But wait, save those tears. An English rose enthusiast, Mr Gordon Rowley (to whom I am indebted for the colour photographs of Lady Mary and of Crimson Glory which adorn this book), on the staff of one of our big horticultural research institutes, heard in 1957 of a reputed Lady Mary Fitzwilliam growing in a back garden of a London suburb. He checked—and found it was indeed a Lady Mary, planted there thirty years before by an amateur enthusiast who was interested in old roses. Later one other plant was found in Ireland—and another 'unconfirmed' Lady Mary Fitzwilliam in New Zealand. Delightedly, Mr Rowley set about re-establishing the great lady in her proper place. Bud-wood was sent to a leading British nursery, Harkness's, who specialised in restoring old varieties.

It took a few years to restore the stock from the three sticks of bud-wood originally available but now Lady Mary Fitzwilliam, the rose that was almost lost to the world, is growing again. And I have no doubt that it will never again be allowed to get so near to extinction. For as Kordes says 'Even if it is a poor grower, it has a wonderful flower and as a parent it has been invaluable.'

I was interested enough in this romance of a rose aristocrat to find out who the real-life Lady Mary Fitzwilliam was. She was a nineteenth-century lady-in-waiting to the German court of Saxe-Coburg. She died in 1929 at the age of eighty-three. As grand an old lady as the rose which bears her name.

26

Sports

A sport, in the horticultural sense, simply means a variation in the varietal norm. It can be a change in colour, habit of growth, even size. It is, briefly, one of nature's accidents. What are the chances of such a thing happening in your garden? That would take a better mathematician than I to work out. But the odds must be fantastic against you—or anyone else—waking up one morning and finding, say, a beautiful scented white bloom appearing on one of your plants of Ernest H. Morse.

Over the years I have had millions, many millions of roses of all types growing under my care. Some, like the brilliant scarlet, short-growing single floribunda Sarabande, seem to delight in 'sporting' as an oft-repeated joke, usually showing one stem of flowers striped red and pink or red and white, like one of the old *gallica* shrub roses. Nothing there, my beauty, to excite my interest for further propagation and possible perpetuation.

Of all the roses it has been my fortune to possess, however temporarily before they were passed into someone else's charge, only one—the Queen Alexandra rose, raised by the present Sam McGredy's grandfather—has ever given a sport that was thought worthy of a place of its own in our catalogues. And that happened as far back as 1927. The Queen Alexandra was a pernetiana (now embraced in the hybrid tea family) of a startling colour combination: vermilion inside the petals, old gold on the reverse. Rather like our more modern Tzigane or Suspense; certainly clearer in its colour definition than Piccadilly.

It happened one morning on our old nursery at Gedling, that one plant of Queen Alexandra was seen to carry just one stem of a flower startlingly different. This bloom was orange-yellow on both sides of the petal, but each petal had a rim of bright cerise pink, as though the colour had been brushed there by a master-artist. This one indeed looked like being a winner. And that one stem was carefully carried to our budding ground for development. Four plants were produced from it to flower next season, all with the same new colouring, firmly fixed. It even seemed a better grower and more hardy than the old Queen—qualities quite possible in a sport. We persevered with it and after putting it on public display in a big way at all the shows in 1927, we put it on sale. Its name: Princess Elizabeth, after the new baby princess who is now our Queen. She sold quite well that first season; some 12,000 plants. Not enough to justify a lengthy run in the catalogues these days but satisfactory enough then. And we were still selling Princess Elizabeth until a new stronger grower of similar colour, Haisha, came to take its place after the war.

Sporting, of course, is no new phenomenon. And obviously the longer the original variety lasts in general cultivation the better is the chance of some really worthwhile sport emerging from it. Peace has produced several—including the beautiful Chicago Peace, found in 1962 in America, and the unusually-coloured Kronenbourg (it's named after a beer!) which originated in McGredy's gardens in Northern Ireland in 1965.

A freak stem from the scarlet and gold bicolour Tzigane gave us the copper coloured Val Boughey. The floribunda Alison Wheatcroft is a Circus sport. Pink Favourite has given us Honey Favourite. The white Frau Karl Druschki even developed a red Druschki.

Piccadilly, the red and orange bicolour, has now sported on the nursery of our Nottingham neighbour Bardill, and a pure yellow Piccadilly is now on the market as Pamela's Choice. Almost simultaneously there occurred another near-yellow Piccadilly, now marketed as Super Sun. My Choice, that luscious beauty from Edward Le Grice, has also taken it into its sweet head to 'go yellow' and a yellow My Choice is now available as Golden Choice.

The cool, classic beauty of Ophelia.

That attractive variety Candy Stripe, which we have featured   28
in our show displays for a number of years, is a pink and white
striped sport of the more familiar Pink Peace (nothing like Meil-   28
land's famous variety from which it was bred but a beauty in its
own right). The tall floribunda Queen Elizabeth has sported   4
several times—most notably to produce a rather pale washy-
coloured Yellow Queen Elizabeth. Incidentally, Scarlet Queen
Elizabeth isn't a sport but a seedling from the older variety.

But the champion sport enthusiast of all time must surely be that
exquisite beauty Ophelia, introduced, from a chance seedling, as
far back as 1912 and still worth growing even though she may now
be a middle-aged veteran. Ophelia is recorded as having sported
no fewer than thirty-five times and the propensity has been passed
down to her progeny. The beautiful Madame Butterfly is an
Ophelia sport—and Madame Butterfly herself sported the still
deeper pink Lady Sylvia. There is a White Ophelia, a White Star
and a Westfield Star, all white sports of the blush Ophelia. There
is Yellow Ophelia, marketed as Silvia, and the Ophelia seedling,
Golden Ophelia, also sported to give us the deeper yellow Rose-
landia, still one of the roses most widely grown in Britain for forcing. And most of these also produced climbing sports. Can you
wonder why I sometimes grin at lecture audiences and say 'A good
old sport was Ophelia'. Shakespeare's tragic heroine destroyed herself, but there seems to be no destroying her namesake—thank
goodness.

Industrial Roses

It was one of those sultry late July days, with not a breath of wind, when even to walk around in my air-cooled office seemed a major effort. A party of visitors was being shown over our rose fields while the budding teams were at work. Now the budders are those nimble-fingered experts who 'make' the new rose plants for us to sell the following year, extracting a bud, or eye, from the required cultivated variety and inserting it beneath the outer skin, the rind, of the wild stock.

In the production of bush trees, those eyes have to be inserted in the neck of the wild rose root, just below soil level. So it follows the budders have to spend hours, days, weeks, bent almost double. It is back-aching work before you get used to it, requiring not only specialist skill but also some physical fitness. Certainly it is no job for anyone with the slightest suspicion of a hangover!

Each budder has an assistant to help him 'tie in', to bind the cut briar stems, either with dampened raffia or with a tiny rubber shield, so that the inserted bud stays fresh and secure under the rind while it knits with the stock that will be its future root system. Each of those two-man budding teams can insert between 1,000 and 1,500 buds a day, all potential saleable plants the following year. That, to the inexperienced, may seem a fantastic rate of progress but with, perhaps, a million and a half stocks requiring to be

It takes all these, and more, to grow your roses.
Some of the staff at Edwalton.

The back-breaking job of budding.

dealt with, there is no scope for laggards.

All this was explained to our visitors. 'But how many of them live?' asked one intrigued young woman.

'Oh, ninety per cent of them, if we're lucky,' I replied.

'Oh but I didn't mean the plants, I meant the men,' she answered. I had to admit that I had no statistics of the casualties on that score—except that it was a job I used to do, year after year, and that even today I had no physical disabilities to speak of.

When I started growing roses commercially, fifty years or more ago now, every single operation in their cultivation had to be performed manually, by sheer hard work, from dawn to dusk, every season of the year, come rain, snow, or heatwave. The ground the stocks were to occupy had to be dug by hand. On our first pocket-sized nursery there was not even a small motorised plough or cultivating machine available. The briar stocks, in their thousands, had to be hand-planted; $7\frac{1}{2}$ inches from each other, in rows three feet apart, just as our neighbouring farmers set out their own small plantlets for a field of cabbages.

All the subsequent attentions; the hoeing to keep down the weeds; the removal of a few inches of soil from around the stem-neck of each briar to expose the spot where the budders would work; the waterings with a hosepipe to ensure that the briars were fresh and thriving, with the sap flowing freely through their veins; all had to be carried out by hand, hard work and excusable oaths. Then came the back-bending weeks of budding.

In the spring, what we call the 'heading back', which is removing the top of the briar stock, leaving the inserted bud alone to grow on the briar roots, had to be done by hand. Then came more hoeing and sucker-removing, each repeated several times during the season. In the autumn of the following year, the rose bushes had to be dug up by spade and loaded into a cart for transportation back to the shed where we assembled them, inspected them and shortened the longest stems, before bundling them and packing them into parcels for dispatch to the customers. Every single job in the cycle was manual and time-consuming.

Now all that has changed. On a modern nursery, specialising in rose-production, this is the machine age. We can't yet say of our roses that they are 'untouched by human hand' but comparatively speaking it is almost so. As I walk round our nurseries—the firm of

A tractor at work cleaning between the rows of cultivated varieties growing in the nursery beds.

A stock-planting gang at work. First a general view of the team; then placing the stocks in the revolving planting wheel; then the stocks after being mechanically planted, firmed and earthed-up.

Harry Wheatcroft and Sons claims to be one of the most highly mechanised rose-growing establishments in Europe—I never cease to look back with wonder on the conditions under which we produced our roses when I was a young man.

It is not exaggerating to say that the tools we now have to grow our roses, and the further tools and buildings we have installed to handle the roses when they are grown, must represent a capital outlay of almost £100,000. Not one of these installations is a gimmick. Every one is there because the need for it has been made ·obvious and because its efficiency has been proven. The sole aim is to grow more and better roses, with the greatest possible savings in money and labour.

Six powerful tractors are the basic work-horses of our 250-acre establishment. Pulling multiple ploughs, they do the preliminary digging. They haul the harrows which level the land and the distributors which spread manure and fertiliser to enrich it. Even the planting of the briar stocks is now mechanical. Four men sit behind the tractor-pulled machine, feeding the briar seedlings into a revolving plate which plants them the required $7\frac{1}{2}$ inches apart and firms each one individually in the ground. Between them, each team of four can set more briars in a day than forty bending, groaning, men would have done in my younger days. A million and a half briars are set in no time—or so it seems. Tractor-drawn hoes keep the ground between the growing plants clear of weeds and there are chemicals, unheard of in my young days, to prevent new crops of seedling weeds springing up, in that seemingly endless succession I used to know only too well. Overhead irrigation systems, laid on to all the rose fields, have taken the place of the old rubber hosepipe, with its kinks and leaks.

There is a machine called a bed cleaner, a sort of giant, horticultural vacuum cleaner, that not only clears any rubbish that might have accumulated round the stems of the briars, but also blows away the top few inches of soil so that the briar necks, fresh and clear, are there awaiting the budders' knives. Power-operated blades, like elongated mechnical hedge-cutters, head back the briars in due course. Behind them comes a machine to collect the severed heads; to grind them into a green mash and scatter the pulp back on to the soil, so that none of the available plant nutrients are lost. The same two machines operate in the same way when the

Part of the automatic irrigation system watering stocks.

A bed cleanser at work; and the job well done.

After the heading-back machine has done its job. The topped stems can just be seen through the snow on the right of the machine which has not yet dealt with the rows on the left.

plants receive their first trimming, in the nursery field, before lifting.

In the meantime, any required spraying has been done by power-driven jets. The lifting itself is done by machine, a kind of plough, with a specially designed extra-broad share with prongs behind, deeply set so that it slides beneath the main root system and lifts the trees out of the ground. All that remains then is for the men to collect and bundle them.

Back the rose-plant harvest comes, in long flat wagons, tractor-hauled, to the receiving and dispatching sheds and here, too, machines now rule. Every wagon bears plants of exactly the same variety, to safeguard customers against the annoying chance of having a wrongly-named specimen among their orders. The wagons are off-loaded on to a conveyor belt for the plants' final treatment before they leave our nursery.

Our sharp-eyed plant inspectors, the most discerning, experienced rose men on our staff, examine each plant as it reaches them to see that it is a first-class specimen, worthy to do justice to itself, and us, when growing in the garden of a customer. Any plant that fails to meet their approval—and we have always insisted on even more stringent requirements than the recently introduced British standard specifications for rose trees—is out. The orders we have given to our inspectors are specific: 'You are the customers' representatives now, not ours. You must not pass anything you would hesitate to buy yourselves.'

The trees, after their appraisal, are stored in racks; compartmented and named according to variety, to be kept in what we call the cold-store, until they are withdrawn as the orders are filled. It is called the cold store but, in fact, the temperature of the storage room is controlled, usually by refrigeration, to stay at just a degree or so above freezing point. From experience we know that rose-trees kept in such conditions will be as fresh and as full of life in March and April as they were when they came in from the fields five or six months previously. Having our plants safely in store means that we can fulfil orders irrespective of the weather. No longer are we forced, as we were in the old days when lifting had to be done manually, to suspend operations when heavy frost is in the ground or the rain is pouring down.

Each order is individually assembled, the required plants once

On the nursery of Harry Wheatcroft and Sons

A field of stocks

A colourful field

29

Sutter's Gold (*photo Downward*)

**Summer Sunshine.
Above, a bloom.
Below, a bed in
Regent's Park**
(*photo Downward*)

The trial grounds
of the Royal
National
Rose Society

The biggest rose
in the world,
Goliath

**Queen Mary's Rose Garden,
Regent's Park**
(*photos Downward*)

33

Princess Mary's Rose Border,
Royal National Rose Society

Left, Gary Player

Right, Alec's Red

Oriana

35

Duke of Windsor

more having to pass an inspector's scrutiny before being bunched and tied by a mechanical bunching machine. Tops are cut back to make an even parcel, the lot are then sewn into a lined paper sack, to be addressed and sent by rail or post to the customer's home.

The same efficient streamlining that has been achieved in the production department has been reached on the office side. Computer aids make the job, if not fool-proof, at least as near to it as modern methods, personal interest and attention to detail, backed by all the skill and know-how of experienced plantsmen, can devise. I do not think it is too much to say that in our organisation every man and woman is just as much a rose lover as the person for whose garden their products are destined and I am sure that applies equally to most rose-growing nurseries the world over. The true nurseryman is not satisfied with his labours unless his customers are.

Now, has the mechanisation of rose-growing been of any practical benefit to the customer, as well as the producer? My firm conviction is that it has, in that it has enabled us to produce top-class plants, plants that we know will grow and give pleasure for years to come, more cheaply than would have been possible if every production operation still had to be done by hand. You can buy first-class plants of first-class varieties from reputable nurseries, even today, for five shillings each. And that, on comparative money values, is less than they were costing before the last World War.

The only possible disadvantage to a customer that I can see is that, in the interests of efficient handling, we have had to reduce the number of varieties we grow. With the best will in the world, we could not handle 750 varieties as economically as we can handle, say, 250. It has meant abandoning any variety proved to us, after trials, to have been bettered by a subsequent introduction, as well as a few old favourite varieties which have stood the test of time but for which popular demand has, temporarily perhaps, slackened.

With so many first-class varieties from which to choose we just cannot afford to keep in commercial production any variety, new or old, of which we cannot sell at least 5,000 plants a year. Customers' preference, not necessarily ours, dictates our yearly budding programme. A lot of the abandoned old-timers I am happy to keep as a source of perpetual enjoyment in my own garden. So budding material is always at hand for the nursery if need be, but

F

even apart from that I would not be without them for the world.

All nurseries, of course, do not adopt the same policy. Nor have they need to. But then not all nurseries have the same basic approach as we have. Some of them use *Rosa multiflora* for their understocks. That, initially, gives a bigger, stronger plant, less prone to suckers, than trees budded on *Rosa laxa*, which we prefer. But *laxa* trees last twice as long, transplant more satisfactorily, and give flowers of much better quality, freedom and texture than is possible from the same variety budded on *multiflora*. We use *Rosa canina* for late budding, but it suckers rather freely, hence our real preference for *R. laxa*.

Scented Roses

Colour, Conformation and Constitution. Those are the three C's I criticise when judging a new seedling variety during what ship-builders would call its acceptance trials. If it passes with honours on these three counts I am reasonably certain we are on to a win-ner. Only after that do I look for fragrance. If the newcomer has that too—wonderful. If not, well, it's still a fine rose if it comes successfully through my 'C' trials.

The Royal National Rose Society, in its marking system for the assessment of trial ground awards, sets a possible maximum of 100 points, a total never yet achieved by any variety. Twenty points each are awarded for freedom of flowering and resistance to disease. Ten points each are awarded for vigour, habit of growth, beauty of form, colour, general effect—and fragrance. Add those necessary ingredients together, and you will see that my yardstick—colour, conformation, constitution—accounts for 90 per cent of the points; fragrance only ten.

The marks, by the way, are awarded by the Society's judging committee, consisting of twenty members with an amateur chair-man. Four members, working on rota, inspect the varieties under test every week from late June till September. Every judge—and I have the honour to be one of them—makes his report separately. To qualify for the award of a trial ground certificate, a seedling must obtain a minimum of 70 points, assessed through the season, and a minimum of 50 per cent must be attained under each heading—excepting fragrance.

Now why should fragrance, which can give so much added enjoyment, be regarded as almost an incidental consideration? It is because a rose which has even a strong scent would be useless as a garden plant if it fell short on the other essentials. Besides, scent, or rather the detection and appreciation of it, is a personal thing. Few people, in my opinion, agree entirely on the extent to which a variety is perfumed; even, in some instances, whether it is perfumed at all.

Our old friend Super Star is a case in point. Some people call it markedly scented—in the American-published standard work, Macfarland's *Modern Roses*, it is recorded as having a strong, fruity fragrance. Others say it exudes a faint, pleasant smell of fresh apples, which, according to my nostrils, is the scent of sweet briar. But there are as many who insist that Super Star is without perfume at all.

Fragrance, in any case, is known to be dependant on a number of outside factors; temperature, for instance, and the degree of humidity. Some authorities say that the ideal conditions for the production and appreciation of scent exist on a mild, airless morning, with the sun warming up after overnight rain. That, I think, explains why some varieties which appeared to have at least a moderate scent in the gardens of their raisers, notably in the South of France, have failed to offer anything, even to the most perceptive nose, in the usually chillier environment of Britain. And why some, like Peace, are usually regarded as being almost scentless out of doors in Britain but undoubtedly have some fragrance when grown under glass.

Scent is caused by a chemical reaction, usually brought about by the weather, on the essential alcohol present in the growing tissues of the rose. That alcohol is contained in the leaves, stems, even in the moss-like hairs of the plant, but is usually most concentrated in the petals. Sometimes—and this makes the question of fragrance all the more intriguing—it is at its maximum when the flower is half-opened; sometimes when the petals are spread wide, drinking in the sun's warmth. Some varieties, such as Crimson Glory, are known to change even the *kind* of scent they exude according to the stage of their flower's development. Crimson

Glory, according to most people who have studied flower fragrance scientifically, first offers the traditional heady scent of its *Rosa damascena* ancestors, then changes to clove.

According to some scientific observers, there are seven basic rose scents: rose, meaning that of the damask rose; nasturtium; orris; violet; apple; lemon and clove. Others list as many as twenty-five. Certainly, it is acknowledged that some varieties may have a combination of scents. But for myself, I am content to leave the problem of all the whys and wherefores in this particular instance to the back-room boys. I'm just content to bury my head in a bloom of Fragrant Cloud or Papa Meilland and thank heaven for the pleasure.

As I have already said, it is impossible to breed for fragrance with any certainty. Two unscented parents can produce scented offspring; two highly scented ones can give us a seedling with no 'nose' at all. One authority insists that only 10 per cent of all the seedlings raised throughout the world each year has any pronounced scent and I would say that that assessment is about right. But it is completely untrue to argue—as some people do—that the modern rose has lost its scent. There are more scented roses available today, if the gardener wants them, than ever there were. Before me at this moment is a catalogue issued over ninety years ago by one of the biggest firms then in the rose-growing business. Only a dozen roses in a list of almost two hundred are recorded as having any appreciable scent. So much for the myth that our roses don't smell like those of grandmama.

Just how important is scent to the average rose gardener anyway? I wonder, because so often when potential buyers visit our nurseries, it is colour, not scent, which is the deciding factor in their choice. Moreover, I've just been checking on the list of varieties awarded the Rose Society's Clay Cup for fragrance from the time it was introduced in 1925, till the award was abandoned in favour of a wider scheme some forty years later. The award, limited to British-raised seedlings, wasn't made every year; only when a variety was considered to merit it. Twenty-three won the Clay Cup over the years. Only a handful of them—Ena Harkness, Silver Lining, My Choice, Lady Seton and the floribundas Elizabeth of Glamis and Scented Air, have enjoyed much popularity with buyers! Now the Clay Cup has been abandoned in favour of a Henry Edland medal, awarded to a scented rose wherever it was raised.

Now, does the Ena Harkness in your garden exude the rich damask scent it should? I ask because Ena, it has transpired, has become something of a scented freak. We nurserymen just couldn't understand it when we began hearing tales of Ena being completely scentless. We waved them aside as just being the complaint of occasional gardeners whose green fingers had perhaps become tobacco-stained. Then the answer emerged. Some strains of Ena had lost their scent.

The explanation, I think, is that somewhere along the line Ena must have sported a stem of completely scentless blooms. Undetected by the unsuspecting nurserymen, budding eyes must have been taken from that stem to propagate other bushes and so on through the years. So a family of completely scentless Enas emerged and the existence of the two strains is now recognised. Every attempt has since been made to eliminate the unscented strain, for this is a sport that gained nothing, but lost a lot, in breaking away from its parent variety! You may rest assured that today, all Enas sold by the reputable nurseries, are as full of scent as they should be.

If you want the lasting fragrance of roses around you through the year, I suggest you try making your own pot pourri with a plant of the old Provins Rose somewhere in your garden to provide the dried petals. For this is a variety of *damascena* which has the unusual property of retaining aroma in its petals even in a dried state. For more than 650 years it has been the basis of all commerically produced pot pourri. And if you want maximum enjoyment from rose scent out of doors, I suggest you keep such diversions as ten week stock, thyme and tobacco plants for another end of your garden!

The American
Industry

The grindstone-sharpened spade, the Dutch hoe and the secateurs
that were the indispensable tools of the rose nurseryman's trade
when my brother Alfred and I first started out in the business fifty
years ago, are now little more than museum pieces in the big production units where mechanical planting and lifting machines—
even a sunshade-covered bicycle-trolley to transport the budder
down his rows of briars—are the equipment of today. Only the
budding-knife, with its razor-sharp edge, for making the T-shaped
incision in the stem of the briar, so that a bud from the desired
variety can be inserted, remains unchallenged. And even that, I
suppose, may disappear, if bud-transplants can be effected by some
such means as the laser beam.

In the mechanical revolution that has advanced on rose production the Americans have been the pace-setters—and if anyone had
predicted *that* in my hearing when I was young I would have told
him to cool his head in the River Trent. In those days, the only
American product remotely connected with our business was the
ancient model-T Ford in which I used to drive our saleable products, flowers and trees in season, around the markets of the English
Midlands. Rose-growing then was almost exclusively a British or
French, certainly a European, concern. The Americans, apparently
interested in cut-flowers but not in do-it-yourself gardens, had little
to offer us, either in the way of varieties or methods. Or even
enthusiasm. And that was certainly true up to the end of World

War Two. In the National Rose Society's analysis of the best roses for the gardens of Britain in 1947, thirty-six varieties were named and only two of them were American: the pink and gold Los Angeles, raised by Fred Howard and introduced by Howard and Swim in 1916; and its more golden sport William F. Dreer, originating in the same nursery four years later.

But the Americans are a fourth-rate rose power no longer. I believe it was the success Wilhelm Kordes achieved with his Crimson Glory, followed by Francis Meilland's world-wide impact with Peace, that led our friends across the Atlantic to their new Klondyke: the millions of dollars to be picked up in the intricate business of hybridising. No wonder they called one of their earliest and greatest post-war introductions Sutter's Gold—after Sutter's Creek, where gold was first struck in California. Today America is raising roses in a big, big way. And as far as plants for sale are concerned, one firm of growers alone produces 15,000,000—yes fifteen million!—trees a year, employing a labour force of 1,500 men and women in their cultivation.

Compare that with Harry Wheatcroft and Sons, one of the biggest growers and marketing organisations for roses in the United Kingdom. Currently, on a farm as fully mechanised as any in the country, we are producing some 1,500,000 roses a year. That is an achievement of pride and satisfaction to me—undreamed of in the days fifty years back when brother Alfred and I had laboriously to hand-plant 5,000 briars on an acre-patch of riverside ground that is now a housing estate. But even production on our present scale is peanuts to some of the Americans!

But despite this almost astronomical expansion, I doubt if it is all being done just for hard cash. Obviously, with money ploughed into the enterprise on the American scale, production, whether of new roses or of plants for sale, must be maintained at a high level to bring about a return for the investment. High-pressure salesmanship must play its part and I can't quibble at that. It's my line, too! But I'm convinced that the top raisers of America, like those in Britain and on the Continent too, are real rose lovers at heart. None of us could trade packets of detergent with the same success, because our affection just isn't there! And of no one is that more true than the man who raised Sutter's Gold. For this long-stemmed scented beauty came to life through a masterstroke of the hybridist's camel-hair brush performed by Herb Swim, a man who has

30

California. On the right, Herb Swim.

The late Eugene Boerner in the act of hybridising. He carries the necessary tools. In his hand are tweezers, in his apron pocket are scissors, envelopes and camelhair brushes.

given all his working life to roses. And Herb is a perfectionist.

Like everyone else engaged in our cause, he has not yet found the ultimate, or so he says. But I am certain the varieties he has given us, whatever minor defects they may have in his eyes, are sufficient to gain him a place for ever in the centuries-old history of roses. For who, among the gardeners of the world today, has not heard of such Swim creations as Buccaneer, La Jolla, Montezuma, Circus, Mojave, Pink Parfait, Helen Traubel, Summer Sunshine? A total, in all, of more than seventy, and still expanding. Swim is a 'natural', with a born hybridist's touch and sensitivity. Not for him mass-production. 'Twenty thousand seedlings a year is all I can fairly look after,' he says. Yet I swear he gets as many winners as anyone.

But rose-growers everywhere owe a debt of gratitude to the American raisers of today, on whatever scale they operate. With men like Swim, Bob Lindquist, Audey Armstrong, Mike Deering, Walter Lammerts and the late great Gene Boerner, there will be new roses aplenty available for years to come. And, inevitably, some of them will be growing in our gardens, yours and mine.

Mention of Bob Lindquist reminds me of another story. The story of the hybridising freak of the century, when two raisers, operating 7,000 miles apart across the globe, produced almost the same variety from different crosses. One of these was Bob, a fourth-generation nurseryman, born of Swedish parents at Hemet, California, where he now runs the Howard Rose Company. By crossing the German-raised floribundas Floradora (Tantau) and Pinocchio (Kordes) he produced a bright scarlet semi-double which he christened Elsinore. It came on the British market in 1957.

At the same time as he was working on that, Francis Meilland, of Peace fame, was busy in France with another, almost identical bright scarlet, with his own Alain as the seed parent, crossed with the Kordes-raised Orange Triumph. And the Meilland rose, under the name of Moulin Rouge, beat Elsinore to the production gun by some five years.

Now both roses were tested in this country and elsewhere under their different names. And our own National Rose Society awarded gold medals to both. For a year or so both names were printed in capitals in the catalogues of some growers as being highly desirable acquisitions. But then the doubts began to arise. Even rosarians as expert as Mr Bertram Park, honorary editor of the Society's *Annual* and a member of the trial ground committee, seemed to have great and growing difficulty in telling them apart.

'I have had both in my garden for two years, grown on the same stock and under the same conditions. I have seen similar plantings on the Society's trial ground at St. Albans and also at Antibes. In no case have I been able to discern any apparent difference between the two varieties.'

So he wrote in the *Rose Annual* for 1962. And Meilland's themselves thought likewise. The upshot was that plants of both sorts were submitted to a French Ministry of Agriculture scientist for minute examination, even down to the plant cells. His report was that the two varieties were in all respects nearly identical.

At the same time, Messrs D. T. Poulsen, the Danish growers, who had introduced Elsinore into Europe on Bob Lindquist's behalf, also sent plants of each to a distinguished Danish plant biologist. He reported that the difference in morphology, the arrangement of the plant cells, between the two varieties was indeed slight but in his opinion sufficient to make them different.

It was decided to call the results of the two examinations an honourable draw. Both scientists and Messrs Poulsen accepted that though there was some difference between the varieties from a scientific aspect, in practice, whether the judge was a professional rose man or an amateur, they were identical. So it was agreed that the production of Elsinore, the newer variety, should be discontinued and nurserymen everywhere were asked that the name should be withdrawn from their catalogues. Thus ended the greatest millions-to-one-against freak in rose hybridising history: a dead heat! Tough on Bob Lindquist certainly, enough to deter a lesser man. But with new roses produced by the millions in permutations it could happen again.

As Poulsen said in a letter to Mr Park: 'Unfortunately we are convinced it will not be the last time a thing like this will happen. Indeed with all the hybridists of the world working like mad to produce novelties it is genetically possible, not to say certain, to happen again sooner or later.'

Yet all that these two roses had in common, in their immediate pedigrees, was one grandmother—Kordes's hybrid musk Eva, the parent of his own dearly loved Baby Château! And that is only one of the quirks which hybridisers must contend with.

Bob Lindquist and a
rather wind-swept
Harry Wheatcroft.

My Own Hints and Tips

It is an old belief that anyone who continually pores over a medical dictionary ends by convincing himself that he has got some incurable disease. Equally, I am sure the novice rose-grower will be put off completely if he sees a list of all the complaints his trees *might* suffer without unremitting care. The thought of hordes of hideous insects known by such forbidding names as *tetranychus telarius* or *spiligrapha alternata* lying eagerly in wait to descend on precious plants is enough to send him in search of a box of antirrhinums and a few geraniums instead.

The advice I offer to anyone who asks me what insects are likely to make war on his roses is that there may be a few—but to forget about them. Just give the plants an early-season spraying with any good proprietory brand of systemic insectide; repeat the dose after fourteen days and at monthly intervals during the growing season. The great advantage of modern systemic preparations, unknown until a few years ago, is that the plants themselves assimilate the essential insect-killing chemicals into their sap, so that a greenfly, say, taking a bite from a leaf so treated, even a fortnight before, is doomed. Until systemics were devised, spraying had had to be done repeatedly, for a light shower was enough to wash all the active chemicals to the ground. Protection was a never ending job. But no longer.

The time may come when the chemists and plant pathologists between them will manage to devise systemic fungicides, to take long-term care of such rose complaints as mildew, black spot and rust, all of which are now far more worrying to a grower than insect-infestation. Then the growing of good roses will indeed be the simplest of all garden tasks. It very nearly is already.

I have said that I did not intend to make this book in any way a primer of instruction. I do not intend to depart from that intention in this chapter. But I feel it might help if I outline some of the good-growing practices I adopt in my own private garden. In doing so I draw on my memories of the questions repeatedly fired at me at flower shows or on the lecture tours I make across the world.

Next to being asked to solve, instantaneously, such imponderables as 'What is the name of the climber growing over my back porch, it's pink and has seven leaves?' I suppose the query put to me most often is 'Why don't my roses grow like yours, Mr Wheatcroft?'

The answer to that, bluntly, is that there is no reason why they shouldn't. Trying to be helpful, I say 'Well, where have you had them planted, madam? How long have they been in? And where did you get the trees?' And often the answer to that last question provides the clue to the initial problem. For so often the answer is 'Oh, I bought half a dozen at the supermarket when I was getting the groceries.'

Now rose-growing and rose-selling is a highly competitive, highly professional business. Every reputable nurseryman, big or small, stands to live or go bankrupt by the quality of the trees he produces. Whether they flourish or die when they are transplanted into your garden is as much his concern as yours, for those trees are his livelihood. He will guarantee their health; their condition when he dispatched them to you; he will vouch that they are fair specimens of the variety; and that they are true to name. Moreover, he will most often guarantee that they will grow, given fair conditions of cultivation, and is prepared to replace them if they don't. But none of those guarantees is given with most of the packaged plants offered for sale alongside tins of salmon or bottles of sauce.

I have seen hundreds of trees, lying on the counters of chain stores, already so dried out that they must inevitably die. I have seen as many others with unripe wood, often sprouting blanched green-eyed shoots, that will as surely fall victim to the first sharp frost that comes. There is no guarantee that the variety named and so enticingly illustrated on the packet is in fact the variety inside. And there is no prospect whatever of getting any that don't grow replaced.

Moreover, many of them are second-grade trees to start with. They must be or they could not have been forced into those constricting, one-sized polythene prisons. The oldest maxim in the rose-growing business is that you will never get first-class results from second-class trees. As an experiment I have several times planted rows of these 'seconds', as growers call them, in a spare corner of my own kitchen garden, just to see whether, with every professional care and attention, they could be induced to overcome their poor beginnings. Many of those seconds have been stronger than others I have seen on offer at the supermarkets; and by supermarkets I don't mean, of course, the recognised trade-organised garden centres. The result, each time, has been merely to prove to me the truth that it can't be done.

So the first essential I urge on any new grower is to start with plants that will be worth the care you are prepared to give them; rewarding plants, whether you buy them from me, from any of the big nurseries, or from the local general nurseryman round the corner. A genuine rose-grower won't let you down. Now what other golden rules do I insist on in my own garden? I will list them for you, under the particular aspect of cultivation concerned.

PLANTING: This is not quite half the battle in the pleasurable task of growing good roses but it's a long way towards it. Do the job thoroughly. Don't try to set up speed records. I have heard people say 'Oh, I got those two dozen roses in in half an hour.' Frankly, I wonder how that can be done. To make a thorough job, see that the planting holes are big enough—at least twelve inches square. If the roots are growing fan-shaped on the tree when it reaches you, plant them that way. But spread the roots out and make sure the main roots don't cross. There is no point in trying to maintain the long 'anchoring' tap roots at their nursery length. Cut them back, so that they are ten inches long. I believe in tipping back *all* roots, except the fibrous ones, in replanting. Just as stem-pruning encourages new 'eyes' to break, so root-pruning encourages the development of new fibrous feeding roots, those through which the plant takes up the nutriments essential to keep it growing. Plant firmly—but don't stamp the replaced soil down so hard that it resembles a concrete road. It is enough to ensure that there are no air pockets left around the roots and that the tree cannot be rocked by the wind. As a safeguard against air pockets, I always give the tree a few gentle shakes as I am planting, to ensure that the finer soil filters through around the fibrous rootlets. To prevent rocking, I shorten all stems (except of climbing varieties, of course) as I plant, to a foot in length.

How deep do I plant and how far apart? Some authorities assert that the budding union, that knob where the stem meets the roots, should be at least an inch below the surface. I believe in leaving bud unions at ground level. Natural sinkage will always take them down a little; mulchings will cover them further. Because I believe the essential purpose of bedding roses is to cover a bed with flower and foliage, I plant my bushes no more than twenty inches apart, unless they are of stronger growing varieties such as Peace and Eden Rose, which need an extra four inches apart and even more if they are to be encouraged to develop into specimen trees. Tall but upright growers such as Perfecta can be planted at the closer distance.

If you are planting a rose border, remember to set the taller trees at the back. The old gardeners' advice regarding herbaceous borders—to bring a few of the taller growers towards the front now and again to avoid height monotony—does not in my experience hold good when roses are the sole occupants of the ground. The natural growth of a rose, some shoots spreading this way, some that, will effectively dispel any appearance of stiff formality.

Blocks of one variety look best, of course, as well as being more convenient. Besides, if you want to say to someone 'Come and see my Super Stars', it is far more impressive to be able to show them off together, instead of having to say 'Well, here's one; there's another over there and I think there's a third down the bottom of the garden somewhere.' But in advocating the planting of several trees of one variety in a group, I am pre-supposing that the garden is big enough, and the owner's enthusiasm strong enough, for a fair proportion of the space to be made available as rose territory. If planting is to be on a restrained scale, pay the same attention to ultimate heights. Don't worry about whether colours in a mixed collection will clash—rose colours seem to have a natural ability to harmonise—but try, if you can, to keep all the roses by themselves. Our queen of flowers is rightly resentful of the presence of rivals, however lovely, at her shoulder.

If you can manage to get the planting done early in the season so much the better, because autumn-planted trees will have sent out their first new, hair-like roots by the time the worst weather of winter arrives. But don't plant if the ground is too wet, or frosted. Better then to heel the plants into trenches, carefully covering the roots, to await the arrival of better conditions. In practice, roses in Britain can be planted any time from early November to the end of April provided that the weather is 'open'. Spring droughts are the greatest danger to the late planted ones. You may have to water late-set varieties if the soil gets too dry. Don't give them just a sprinkle, an occasional good soaking will be far more effective than any number of mere surface dampings. Whatever the time of planting, roses are always liable to get loosened in their soil hold by the action of hard frosts. Make sure they are firmed again as soon as the frost is over. With those precautions taken, you can let them go—and grow. Which brings me to the next operation in the calendar.

PRUNING: Long or short? Winter or spring? When I first started, there would have been no question. Roses, we were told, should be pruned any time between the middle of March and end of April, depending largely on where in Britain you lived. The further north, the later the date. As for the amount of wood removed, it was always 'Don't be afraid to prune hard. The harder the pruning the better the flowers.' Now, of course, there are advocates of November-December pruning; of the value of getting the whole operation done by January at the latest. And roses, we are told, weren't meant to be pruned as heavily as we used to prune them.

Which school of thought is right? So far as I'm concerned, I can only tell you that this is one of the aspects of rose-growing over which I have remained old fashioned. I still look on mid-March as pruning time, the time when the sap is running and when even the hidden ravages of winter, the stems outwardly sound but internally mortally stricken with frostbite, begin to show themselves. Mid-winter pruning, in some parts of the country, simply means that in two years out of four the job has only to be done all over again in March or April, because of the damage late frosts have done to the

G

Planting. Showing first, a strong maiden plant ready for planting; next, the hole prepared and the bottom filled with a mixture of peat, soil and bonemeal, and showing also the care that is being taken to keep the roots well spaced; then the soil and peat mixture being dribbled back round the roots; and finally, firming the soil round the planted tree. Note the union of stock and bud just above ground level.

Pruning. First, a
standard being pruned;
then, after pruning.
Note the carefully
balanced head and the
necessary open centre.

You will not kill it by
hard pruning. Note the
length of stem being cut
away on a newly planted
rose, to leave four buds
on the stem.

already-pruned stems. So the pruning knife best stays in its drawer until springtime. Besides, cuts made when the sap is running heal much quicker, so reducing any risk of infection.

Now how much wood do I remove from the stems? Everything dead, damaged or weakly growing, of course. Any shoot, however sound, that threatens to interfere with the open centre of the plant. Then, on all varieties except those such as Peace and Eden Rose, known to resent repeated hard pruning, I cut away enough wood to leave only four or five eyes on each stem of the previous year's growth. That way, I believe, you get the best flowers. By all means prune lighter, cutting stems back to say half their existing length, if your primary object is to ensure a mass of colour, irrespective of whether specimen-size flowers occur or not. Floribundas, of course, should always be less severely pruned, after the first year, than hybrid teas.

But whether you prune long or short, here's one tip to adopt with all established trees, whether hybrid teas or floribundas. Always cut at least one main stem back to within two eyes from the base every year. Then you will ensure a continuance of the strong, fat, basal shoots so vital if the plant is not to look leggy and prematurely aged. And while we're still at the pruning stage, let me refer again to frosted shoots. Never, never leave a half-frosted shoot in the hope that it will recover. It won't. It might linger on to bear a sickly-looking flower during the first flush in June or July, but it will go no further. However green a shoot may look externally, cut it back if it shows the slightest sign of browning inside, in the pith. Cut it back until the pith looks as it should, clear and firm and white, like a freshly-sliced apple.

Sometimes, after pruning, you will find that if a main shoot-eye gets frosted or damaged, two smaller eye-buds will appear, one on each side of it. These are what we call guard eyes. They are a natural provision for just such a contingency. Left to grow, both these eyes will develop and you will have two shoots emerging from a common base. This is undesirable and will only complicate pruning. It is best, if you can, to rub out one of these sprouting guard eyes with a finger-nail while it is still in its embryonic stage.

There is another point I am very particular about in my growing calendar. I have told you I prefer spring to winter pruning. I do insist on one other pruning operation.

Be sure to make a slanting cut just above an outward-pointing eye.

Prune as shown on the stem farthest right. The stem on the left has been cut too close to the growing bud. The centre stem has been wrongly cut square instead of at an angle, and also too far above the bud, leaving a snag of wood which will die off as the bud develops.

PARTIAL AUTUMN PRUNING: I think it is one of the fundamentals of good rose garden management to see that any shoots over three feet long, on all hybrid teas and floribundas except the climbing sports, are reduced to near that height at the end of every season, by the end of November at the latest. It helps to ensure against possible damage from the weight of snow, should a heavy fall come. It helps to eliminate the possibility of over-wintering disease. But above all it prevents wind-rocking, the chance that trees will get so tormented by the gusts of winter that they twist and turn in their beds, forming deep pockets in the soil around their main stems. These pockets can quickly fill with water, which can as quickly freeze. And a rose root, it has now been proved, is even more vulnerable than the top-growth to freezing. Besides, autumn-topping makes the eventual spring pruning so much easier.

PESTS: Greenfly, caterpillars (including that infuriating species that causes rose leaves to curl, then hides itself in the folds as though it were in a sleeping bag) and thrips, those minute black flies, almost invisible to the naked eye, that delight in making such an unholy distorted mess of the first flowers of Ophelia and her kins-women, can all be effectively controlled by the same all-purpose systemic insecticide. Buy one of the good proprietary brands and follow the instructions. Never make the spray stronger than the makers advise. You won't kill more bugs. You're more likely to kill, or at least seriously damage, your trees. Almost all other insect pests, common or uncommon, likely to cause damage or disfigure-ment to rose plants can be dealt with by the same spray. I wish remedial treatment were as simple for the complaints encompassed in the next section.

DISEASES: Mildew, black spot, rust, very occasionally, stem canker. Those are the ones you need worry about. All are fungus diseases.
  Canker is caused by damage to a stem through which a fungus enters. If you see a stem where the outer tissue—we call it the rind—has broken or split, revealing a patch that looks gnarled and scaly as though it were a piece of bough from an ancient oak tree, cut it out immediately. For that is stem canker. It can be trans-mitted from plant to plant, possibly by insects. You will find it more often on the stems of climbers that have been subjected to some skin abrasion as a result of a winter's winds. Deal with it

Mildew.

Black spot.

Rust.

promptly—but don't worry about it. I've never yet seen a large scale epidemic.

Of the other three, mildew is the most common and the least dangerous. Because of chemicals in the air, neither black spot nor rust can get a hold on roses grown in urban areas. Mildew can—and it is about mildew that I get most queries on diseases. Warm days, after cooler, dewy nights, are ideal conditions for the fungus, which leaves a white powdery coating on stems and leaves and, in bad infections, even on the calyx of the bud itself. Treatment is comparatively simple. Sulphur is the best-known deterrent. Spray the bushes with a solution based on the sulphur compound known as karathane and the trouble will soon be under control.

Mildew disfigures. Black spot and rust both defoliate—and both, unlike mildew, can overwinter on the plant or on the surface of the soil. I have seen whole gardens, even those under professional care, defoliated by the end of August as a result of heavy black spot infestation—but that, happily, was before the arrival of modern deterrents. The creation of smokeless zones in towns—black spot, as I have said, can only exist in clean air—may have laid many more rose gardens open to possible fungus attack, but the counter-measures now are more effective than they were even five years ago. Black spot, like rust, needs treatment with a copper compound. You will find it, in forms known as maneb or captan, in specific proprietary sprays. Against both diseases I find it a wise precaution to spray initially with a weak solution of copper sulphate, an ounce to a gallon of water, as soon as pruning is completed, before the leaves begin to grow. That should reduce the chances of re-infection from over-wintering fungus spores.

Some people insist that it is not necessary to spray against either black spot or rust until its appearance is actually noted; the presence of tale-telling black spots, like fringe-edged blobs of brown-black ink, on the surface of the leaves in one instance; the bright orange-coloured dots, for all the world like metallic rust, on the underside of the leaves in the other. Larger, rust-coloured spots also appear on the upper surface of the leaves at the outset of some attacks of rust. Both diseases, in my experience, strike first at leaves growing nearest the ground.

Personally, I've always believed in the axiom that prevention is better than cure, although there is not yet a real cure, in the strict sense, for either of these complaints. So I give one spray of a proprietary preparation recommended for use against both diseases in mid-May and continue to spray at fortnightly intervals until the end of August. Believe me, the trouble is worth it.

Now, in these days when labour is scarce and time vital, you may well ask if it is not possible to use insecticide and fungicide preparations in the one combined spray. It is—but first make sure from the makers that the preparations used are compatible, otherwise a chemical reaction may occur that might seriously damage the plants instead of protecting them.

Considerable research is still being done on both rust and black spot by plant scientists in all the major rose-producing countries of the world. It is now established that the incidence of both diseases in really epidemic proportions occurs in cycles of years, just as the 'flu germs which attack humans vary in type and intensity from year to year. Unfortunately, it has not yet been found possible to establish any set pattern for the expected occurrence of really bad black spot years or really bad rust years. In my experience, both diseases persist in varying intensity from year to year in any sizeable rose garden in clean-air surroundings. I fear our chemists have not yet reached the same degree of efficiency with their fungicides that they have with their insecticides. Nor have our breeders, over the years, been as insistent on the production of disease-resistant varieties as they have on the introduction of so-called new colours. But, very recently, one important scientific discovery has been made.

It was thought, until now, that only man and animals could acquire an inbuilt immunity to disease. Now it has been established that plants can, too. So the day may yet come when we have a rose that is, by nature, almost disease-free, certainly highly disease-resistant. Injected serums might also be used, as vaccines are with humans and animals. Until that time, I feel the ball is in the court of the chemists and the breeders. The need is urgent. The task is tremendous. No known rose, either species or cultivar, is immune to rust. Only one, the species *Rosa bracteata*, parent of the climber Mermaid, is, according to American scientists, naturally free from black spot. The fact that Mermaid is almost black spot-proof—particularly fortunate since it usually retains its leaves in all but the severest winters—is perhaps a pointer in the direction some enterprising breeder might take.

FEEDING: I am a life-long believer in the value of organic manures. We use farmyard manure extensively in the rose fields on my nursery. Every established rose bed in my own garden gets a top dressing of it, applied as a thick mulch, every spring. For town-dwellers this may not be so easy, since not everyone can find supplies of natural manure so readily available as we in a farming area can. If I had to do without it, my selected alternative would be an annual mulch of coarse peat moss, bought in bulk for economy. Now peat will supply humus, but not food. So I would apply, at the rate of four ounces to a square yard, a chemical feed consisting of twelve parts by weight of superphospate of lime; ten parts by weight nitrate of potash; two parts sulphate of magnesia; one part sulphate of iron; eight parts sulphate of lime. This is the formula for that time-proven old tonic known as Tonks' fertiliser. Some growers I know swear by a formula consisting of six parts by weight potassium nitrate; three parts amonium sulphate; sixteen parts superphosphate of lime; six parts potassium sulphate. An application of either, at the four ounce to a yard rate, in early May, followed by another in mid-June and a third not later than the end of July, should provide all the essential nutrients: there are several proprietary rose foods on the market which employ much these formulas. But do not rely on chemicals to the complete exclusion of humus-forming material. To do so would soon impoverish the soil and your roses would flounder, not flourish. Don't give artificial feeds later than July or newly induced growth may not ripen. And don't be heavy-handed with purely nitrogenous foods. Roses may be greedy feeders—but you *can* over feed them, when coarse growth and fewer flowers will result. The average rose bush would much rather have a meal of potash than one of nitrogen.

To ensure freedom of flowering, I dead-head regularly, cutting off the spent flowers to a new eye growing some three to four inches below. It is never good policy to cut too many long-stalked blooms from any one tree in one season. And I insist that no long stalks are cut at all from my bushes during the first season after planting. The aim then must be to build up a strong healthy bush for the future. And the tree needs those long shoots far more than the lady of the house does!

SUCKERS: I deal with these promptly and regularly. Just what is a sucker? It is a briar growth, emerging from the stock on to which the cultivated variety was budded. It may come from the roots, or it may come from the main stem, below the so-called budding union. That is the actual site of the bud insertion and you can identify it on your plants as the rather knob-like protuberance placed just above the roots, from which the actual branches spring. Any shoot growing from or above that budding union is part of the rose—certainly not a sucker.

Those sucker shoots growing from the main-stem beneath the union should be rubbed off at the base. Those emerging from the roots should be traced back to their point of origin by carefully scraping the soil away, then giving the offending sucker a sharp tug. *Never prune a sucker*, not, at least, at ground level. The effect is the same as if you had pruned a shoot. The operation merely induces new, even more vigorous, growths. Suckers are below-ground shoots natural to the wild rose, and have the same two guard-eyes that flowering eyes from the cultivated stem possess. Injure the first, as you do with ground-level pruning, and you have its two watchdogs as well to contend with. If you *tear* that sucker away from its moorings, more often than not you will manage to pull the guard-eyes away with it too.

What causes suckers? A variety of things. Insecure planting is one. The rose sends up added supports from its roots to help anchor itself. Damage to the root system, caused by over-deep hoeing or other forms of cultivation is another. So never dig round roses but gently prick the bed surface over with a border fork, going no deeper than an inch or, at the most, two inches. Some stocks used for budding are naturally more prone to suckering than others. Every nursery worth its salt still insists on the closest inspection of bushes before they are despatched to the customer to make sure no embryo suckers are developing. If they occur afterwards, as some will, it is in your own interests to see that they are removed immediately. I am often being told 'Oh, it was a good rose once but it quickly went back to briar'. That is nonsense. No rose goes back to briar just like that. Only when the suckers are allowed to grow, stifling the cultivated variety, robbing it of nourishment. And for

A sucker being traced
back to its point of
origin from the roots.
(The knife is being used
simply to point to the
actual junction.)

This is a sucker emerging
from a *rugosa* standard
and is about to be pulled
off at its point of origin.

that, don't blame the rose. Blame the gardener!

There is one other phase of growing on which I might be able to give a few tips, gained from long and sometimes disappointed experience.

EXHIBITING ROSES: I do not mean those in the 'twelve specimen varieties, all different' classes that test the strength of our top professionals and amateurs at many of the leading shows. I mean the exhibits requires from competitors at local district shows or village fêtes.

In a class for decorative roses—or, in the smaller shows, for roses of any kind—eye-catching arrangement of the blooms is all important. If, say, three roses in a vase are required, don't pack three in one line. Have two at the back, one in front. If six roses are needed, have two in the back row, three in the middle and one in front. Try to get an evenness, a symmetry of line, with all the companion blooms. The usual custom, for roses shown in vases, is for them all to face the front.

Roses shown in bowls should be placed to face all round—and more experienced judges do, in fact, move the bowl around to ensure that they do. My advice for bowl showing is to set your roses in pairs. Arrange the two with the longest stalks at the same time, setting them at opposite ends of the bowl, in line. Then fill in the middle with the others matched according to stem length. Use those with the shortest stems for the front and back of the bowl. Harmony of colour is important; so is equal spacing between the various blooms. Look at the whole exhibit from the point of overall effect.

If I were showing in these classes—and I was doing so once—I would prefer to cut the roses the day before the show and keep them in a dark, cool, airy place overnight. Always pick 'spares' in case a first-choice bloom gets too full blown to show. Always strip all the thorns from the lower half of the stems, but keep the foliage intact. In some classes, the health of the foliage displayed is taken into points-winning consideration. 'Dressing' a bloom is permissable in these decorative classes, by which I mean the careful removal of, say, a broken petal. But be careful not to over-dress; and don't handle the flower itself any more than is necessary. The 'bloom' can rub off a rose petal, just as easily as it can from a grape.

Making the Most of Your Roses

In the Nottinghamshire village of Caunton, twenty miles from my home, there is a gravestone in the parish churchyard which says simply: 'Here rests Samuel Reynolds Hole, D.D., vicar of Caunton, 1850–1887, Dean of Rochester, 1887–1904; born Dec. 5, 1818, died Aug. 27, 1904'.

It is a plain enough memorial to a great man; a man whose achievement, briefly, was to teach the whole world to love roses. For it was Dean Samuel Reynolds Hole who 'fathered' the National Rose Society in Great Britain, now honoured with the prefix Royal, the biggest institution of flower-lovers in the world. The Society began in 1867; Hole became its first president. But eighteen years before that he had organised Britain's first rose show. Two thousand people came to see the displays of teas and noisettes and hybrid perpetuals—hybrid teas were still unknown—and, as Hole says in his classic *Book About the Rose*, published in 1901, 'I went to bed that night as tired, as happy, and, I hope, as thankful as I had so much cause to be.'

I wonder what the venerable old gentleman would have said today—when the production, and sales, of our rose nurseries is almost 50,000,000 trees a year (almost half America's output, for all its size) and when our Royal National Rose Society numbers more than 118,000 members as against only 15,000 in its American counterpart.

Dean Hole, the founder of the Royal National
Rose Society—he now has 118,000 followers.

Now why should I be thinking especially of the worthy Dean as I write this chapter on roses in the landscape or, more precisely, on landscaped rose gardens? Simply because Dr Reynolds Hole prescribed, in his book, the requirements of an ideal rose garden as he visualised one, and I can think of no better prescription:

'There should be beds of roses, banks of roses, hedges of roses, edgings of roses, baskets of roses, vistas and alleys of roses.'

Dr Hole, like so many authorities of his time, believed firmly in the virtue of having a garden devoted exclusively to the culture of the rose—'but no formalism, no flatness, no monotonous repetition should prevail.'

The skilfully landscaped rose garden of the 1970s must equally be no set pattern of stiff geometrical shapes but a thing of softness, variation, even surprise.

The rose for the garden or the garden for the rose? You may argue that in this age of pocket-sized enclosures it is space-wasting to set aside one part, however tiny, for the exclusive occupancy of any one flower. I do not agree. In my opinion, and this the accumulated experience of half a century, roses do infinitely better on their own than as competitors, however willing, for space and air with assorted phloxes, michaelmas daisies, golden rods and herbaceous what have you. Give your roses a place of honour, even if it is just one bed, and you and they will benefit.

Now if you are ambitious, as I hope, and decide to make an exclusive rose garden, what advice can I give you?

First, draw your intended design on paper—to scale if possible. Start with a focal point, a central feature: a seat, a bird-bath, a sundial, a stone figure, what you will. Make your pattern of beds flow out, from and around it. Do not make beds too small—the effect will look spotty. Or too big or you will forever be treading on carefully-hoed soil. An ideal bed-size, in my opinion, is nine feet by five feet to hold twenty bushes of average hybrid tea or floribunda growth.

Keep the shapes simple—square, oblong, circular. The arabesques, pointed stars, Adam-esque scrolls and quartermoon shapes so beloved of old-time gardeners as sites for their precious summer bedding plants are out. They may look wondefrul on paper. But, in practice, there is too much wastage of space when roses are the

Summer Holiday
(*photo Walter Gregory*)

Rose Gaujard
(*photo Downward*)

Femina

Prima Ballerina

Manuela

Stella

Beauté

Piccadilly. Above, a bloom
Below, in the mobile greenhouse, a
week before the Chelsea Show

Memoriam

Royal Highness

bed-occupants. Besides, edge-trimming and cutting is so much more difficult, particularly if a power-driven machine has to be manoeuvred round the course! If you plan a rose-border, say against a fence or wall or even as an island site, it will look better curved, with a bay or bow window shape, than straight.

Cloak that fence or wall with some of the beauties from among the perpetual flowering climbers. If you wish, break the flatness of a large bed with selected standards, or with climbers again, the pillar rose type, trained on single larch poles. Make hedges, five feet or more tall, of the most vigorous varieties of hybrid teas—Uncle Walter, Buccaneer, Dame de Coeur—or of floribundas like Queen Elizabeth, Dorothy Wheatcroft, Honeymoon or Elysium.

Bowers of roses? They can be made with a simple broad square-shaped arch, again planted with the choicest climbers. Choose fragrant ones, if you can, for scent in a bower is scent from heaven. Plan a pergola, with more climbers, as a paved walk or as a dividing line from the rest of the garden.

Banks of roses? You can have these, too, if you have a retaining bank to cope with—or decide to build one for the special purpose. Don't grass that bank down; plant long, loose-caned climbers there for a change. Let them spread, wander at will. Or use some of those old hybrid teas like Hugh or George Dickson, damask-scented, deep-glowing reds, both of them, with their long shoots pegged down in graceful arcs. A novel idea? No, something we used to do regularly and effectively in the old days.

Now, a question I am always being asked: is it better to have the varieties 'all mixed up' or to keep them in separate blocks? Let no one deny these mixed plantings can, and do, make a wonderful kaleidoscope of colour. But, personally, I prefer the massed effects obtained when several plants of the same sort are grown together. A whole bed of one variety is most effective of all. Pruning is simplified and there are or should be no height problems.

Be careful, with all your plantings, to study the ultimate heights. Have you ever sat in a cinema, trying desperately to peer over the head of a six foot six man in the seat in front? It must be like that for poor little Doreen if you should be so misguided as to plant her behind a towering Queen Elizabeth or even a Rose Gaujard, of more normal stature.

The rose, more than any other flower, seems to have a happy

H

Bettina / Golden Treasure

Super Star   Paprika

Kings Ransom

E.H.Morse   Queen Elizabeth

Piccadilly   Oh La La

Fragrant Cloud   Iceberg

Tip Top

Make a plan of your plantings.

Large beds usually look best curved

Front Garden   The Queen Elizabeth

Alison Wheatcroft
Iceberg
Oh La La

All Gold

Fragrant Cloud

Tip Top

Paprika

Maigold

Pink Parfait   Tip Top

An idea for a corner

You can use roses in all kinds of ways.

114

There is no reason why your arches should not look like this—if you have room.

Pegging down—using roses as ground cover.

14, 7, 10

43, 18

ability to blend its varied colours. But there can be clashes Don't set Papa Meilland, for instance, next to Fragrant Cloud or Wendy Cussons. Or two reds together, even two yellows. Use your yellow to offset your reds. A bicolour, like Piccadilly or My Choice, is always a useful 'merger'.

Grass paths or stone slabs? That eminent eighteenth-century landscape artist Lancelot (Capability) Brown, still regarded as the supreme master of his craft, insisted on curves instead of straight lines—not for him those long martial avenues of trees that were ducal drives in days gone by. Brown wouldn't have flowers in his landscapes either. He is said to have thought the colours 'too strident'. Green it had to be for him every time. And there, in my landscaping, I agree with him, at least on that one point. Give me green as a setting for my roses, every time. Grass paths and lawns instead of concrete or stone slabs, however much drier these may be underfoot on a typical English summer's day. Flag the pathway under the pergola, yes. But a natural carpet everywhere else, please.

So, go to your landscaping with a will. Plan your plans. Plant your plants. In squares, circles, oblongs, half-moons, you will find the rose won't let you down. But no violas, aubretias, pansies or even spring bulbs to keep her company. Let the Queen reign without attendants. But you can if you wish, and I suggest you do, introduce a few four feet specimens or upright-growing conifers—*Cupressus elwoodii*, *fraseri* or *fletcheri* are best—set among the turf, like dark, evergreen sentinels, and our vista of charm and elegance will be complete. If you need a hedge or windbreak, other than roses, I suggest *Cupressus leylandii*. It looks as effective as yew, is much quicker to grow, is easy to trim—and doesn't send any greedy invasive roots to rob the roses of their sustenance.

31, 33, 34

Visit the gardens of the Royal National Rose Society at St Albans, or Queen Mary's Rose Gardens in Regent's Park, London, to see just how roses should be displayed.

My own experience of landscaping reminds me of a coincidence. The man who set my brother Alfred and me off as garden-designers, away from our jobs as plodding nurserymen, was called Tyler, a Nottingham cigar manufacturer. He came to us one day and asked if we would lay out his entire new garden, complete with rose garden, lawns, trees, shrubberies, the lot, even a hard tennis court.

And—the coincidence—it was in a town called Tyler, in Texas, that I came across what I still think must be the most enthusiastic collection of rose-growers, at least numerically, I have ever seen. Every day I spent there it was impressed on me that Tyler, with a population of around 50,000, boasted twenty-five millionaires— and twenty-five million rose trees! Not even Dean Hole's beloved Nottingham can surely equal that. Though it was of my birth-place that the Dean wrote:

'No town in England displays the gardening spirit more mani-festly than 'old Nottingham'. Independently of gardens attached to residences, there are, it is said, nearly 10,000 allotment holders within a short distance of the town; and as many of these are divided, and in some cases sub-divided, it is not too much to affirm that from 20,000 to 30,000 of the inhabitants, or nearly one half, take an active interest in the garden. And where will you see such roses?'

Many of those allotments are still there today . . . still growing roses. But—and this I think is utter ingratitude on our part—on that grave in Caunton churchyard no rose grows. Dean Hole had a hybrid tea named after him—a silvery carmine, raised by Dickson of Hawlmark, introduced in 1904, the year he died, and long since out of commercial production. The Royal National Rose Society has an award named in his memory—the Dean Hole Medal. But there is no memorial garden; nowhere for us to find those banks and beds and vistas of which he dreamed, except in our own small corners. I suggest it is time that sad deficiency was put right. Why not a Dean Hole garden—right in the heart of the shire he loved?

The classic beauty of Peace, the greatest ever.

Harry Wheatcroft Selections

Hybrid Teas

Trying to make a short list of the best hybrid teas is difficult. I think I have seen every new variety of any consequance put into world commercial production in the last fifty years—as well as thousands that fell by the wayside. Eliminating the worthwhile from those we can forget is easy. But to try to cut down my champion hybrid teas to a few dozens is like trying to reduce the extent of the average family's Christmas card list. However drastic the intention, you find so many names you just cannot leave out.

I can claim to have tested, either on the Wheatcroft nurseries or in my own garden, at least ninety-five per cent of all the varieties which are named in the select list which follows. The remaining five per cent are new introductions which, at the time of writing, I have only seen on trial in other people's grounds. But I have used their opinions and my own, now well-seasoned, judgement to select from among them those that I think will figure prominently in our gardens in the 1970s—and even beyond. I have given you what I believe to be the most comprehensive 'what's what' yet assembled about these varieties in any one book. All the details you need to make your own particular choice are there. And you won't, I think, be disappointed however you may permutate among them.

In each instance I have given first the variety's country of origin; then the date of its introduction into Britain; our dates have usually coincided with those of other European countries but there has been some differences between us and America. Then follow the breeder's identity; the variety's parentage (where known, sometimes it's kept a deliberate secret, for fear that others might get ideas!) a description of the flower, including its petal count; the honours it has won; and, finally, a few tips on treatment where I think these may be helpful.

In describing heights, I have taken Ena Harkness as the yardstick—as indeed it is, being three feet tall under average British conditions.

In a very few instances the parentage of a variety is recorded differently in our own National Rose Society's well-chosen select lists, compared with the entry in the American-published world accepted reference book, McFarland's *Modern Roses*. Where this discrepancy exists, usually as to which variety was the seed parent and which provided the pollen, I have chosen to abide by the American version. That is not to doubt the veracity of the enlightened editorial committee of our Society's publication but just in the cause of international clarity.

After drawing up this list, I am more impressed than ever by the extent to which Peace has influenced our latter day varieties; a study you can make for yourself. For my part, I can only say that where I have had to refresh my memory the result has been enlightening. I have found, for instance, another Prima Ballerina— raised by a Russian. I have met that charming lady, Mme Vera Klimenko several times. I did not know, until now, that in 1955 she produced her own Prima Ballerina, under the Russian name of Solistka Baleto! This one is also a Peace seedling—Peace crossed with a seedling obtained from Crimson Glory and Poinsettia. Its flowers are described as large, fragrant, soft lemon-yellow, edged pink.

And talking of Peace. Our Peace, Meilland's great rose, wasn't, I've found, the first of its name. Peace was the title given originally to a creamy-white sport of the pink and lemon tea rose, G. Nabonnand. Like its modern namesake, it came out at the end of a war—the Boer War in 1902. But let us be clear, it's Meilland's Peace, the 1942 introduction, and Tantau's Prima Ballerina I refer to in my list.

There is a new rose, still under trial in my own garden, which I have not mentioned in my selections but which could still be in great demand, especially by exhibitors, in the 1970s. It is a deep-salmon pink, with coral overtones—and it is a giant in every way.

32

The bushes in my trial bed have grown to four feet high in their second year and its blooms are quite the biggest I have ever seen, on any rose. Fully opened, they are seven inches across. Some have been as big as saucers, with wide, long petals reflexing gracefully from high-pointed centres. If it continues to live up to its present promise, I will certainly market it, making it clear that it is an exhibitor's rose only, since, at the moment, it is not quite free enough with its huge flowers for bedding purposes. But, on the show bench, it may prove a real winner. From all appearances so far, I think Goliath will prove an appropriate name for it.

Outstanding in the open field trial ground at our nursery has been a dark-red rose, a daughter of Fragrant Cloud, raised by Alec Cocker, of Aberdeen. All through its extensive trials, here and elsewhere, it has been affectionately referred to as Alec's Red and that, I am pleased to say, is the name under which it is now to be introduced to the market this year. It is of ideal bedding habit; a deep red, unfading flower that is always in bloom, and a strong grower to boot. A variety I can thoroughly recommend which is indeed a credit to its raiser, a newcomer to the business of breeding.

Under nursery conditions, too, a South African-bred bicolour carmine pink with paler reverse, named after their great golfer, Gary Player has given us every satisfaction. Dickson's 1969 gold medal winner Red Planet, scarlet with a paler reverse, looks promising, but lacks scent. For eye-catching beauty I give top honour in our own 1969 trials to a Tantau-raised bicolour, a startling full-petalled rose of deep-ruby red, with silver reverse, not unlike the older Francine, but a better shaped flower and a far better grower. For this one, there has been no affectionate nickname, it has simply been referred to by the number Tantau first gave it on his nursery—number 6446. It is to be marketed this year.

Which reminds me. When I introduced Tantau's brilliant-light vermilion, Duke of Windsor, to Britain two years ago, it was described as a seedling from Prima Ballerina and it is this parentage which the Royal National Rose Society quotes in its official publications. But Tantau now tells me that it is, in fact, the result of a cross between the floribunda Spartan and the grandiflora Montezuma and on his authority this is the pedigree I give for it in my select list.

ALEC'S RED: Scotland, 1970, Cocker; Fragrant Cloud × Dame du Coeur;   **35**
full, medium-sized (4½ in.) flowers of 36 petals, opening cup-shaped; dark
crimson, slightly paler reverse, borne usually in trusses; growth upright,
vigorous and branching; average height; foliage mid-green, glossy. A good
red rose for bedding. Henry Edland medal for fragrance, Britain, 1969.

CHAMPS ELYSEES: France, 1957, F. Meilland; Monique × Happiness;
cupped bloom, 35 petals, rich crimson; below average height but bushy
and vigorous; a first-class garden variety, markedly rain-resistant, seldom
out of flower and always bright; just a whiff of fragrance, if your nose is
keen; foliage matt, pale green, tough.

ENA HARKNESS: England, 1946, Norman; Crimson Glory × Southport;
full bloom, 30 petals, high-centred, crimson scarlet, with no sign of the
blueing which spoils so many varieties of similar colour as the flowers age;
average growth, ideal for bedding; almost rain-proof—in fact at its best in
dull weather; usually a strong damask perfume; one of the all-time greats,
its only fault is a tendency to hang its head; foliage semi-glossy, medium-
green. Gold Medal, N.R.S., 1945; Portland, U.S., 1955.

ERNEST H. MORSE: Germany, 1964, Kordes; Prima Ballerina ×   **15**
Brilliant; tall, high-centred blooms, 30 petals, turkey-red; strongly fragrant; below average height but vigorous and free; easy to grow but needs
to be watched for rust in districts and seasons where this is prevalent;
foliage semi-glossy, dark green. A real acquisition. Gold Medal, N.R.S.,
1965.

EROICA: Germany, 1969, Tantau; parentage unknown; deep-crimson
buds, 30 petals, opening to full, attractive flowers, high-centred with re-
flexing petals; damask-scented. Growth above average height; foliage
dark olive-green, glossy.

JOSEPHINE BRUCE: England, 1949, Bees Ltd.; Crimson Glory ×   **13**
Madge Whipp; broad flower, 25 petals, darkest crimson, yet each fragrant
bloom lit with an iridiscence that makes an eye-catching appeal; growth
slightly below average but sprawling, counteract this by pruning some
shoots to inward-growing eyes; foliage medium green, dull. Needs watching for mildew but worth every care. Dressing with sulphate of potash
(2 oz. per square yard, April and July) helps. Trial ground certificate,
Britain, 1953.

LANCASTRIAN: England, 1965, Gregory; parentage undisclosed;
colour quality and habit all similar to Ena Harkness—except that this one
has the strength in the neck to hold its plentiful blooms upright. It is
strong perfumed, too, so of all Ena's rivals—Mardi Gras, My Love, Red
Ensign—this may be the one to take her place.

11 MME LOUIS LAPERRIERE: France, 1952, Laperrière; Crimson Glory ×unnamed seedling; medium-sized double bloom, 45 petals, rich deep-crimson, heavily-scented; an excellent bedding variety of average growth and exceptional freedom of flower. Virtually trouble-free, this is the one that knocked that old favourite Etoile de Hollande from the lists and has herself reigned unchallenged since. Foliage semi-glossy, medium green, small. What is more, it can stand rain. Gold Medal, Bagatelle, France, 1950; Certificate of Merit, Britain, 1952.

NEW STYLE: France, 1962, A. Meilland; Happiness ×Independence seedling ×Peace; full cup-shaped blooms, 25 petals, tough, leathery, glowing crimson; Peace-type growth and, like Peace, resents too much pruning; trouble-free and rain-resistant. Little scent but if you want a striking splash of dark red for the back of a border, this is the style. Foliage dark green, strong, disease-resistant.

14 PAPA MEILLAND: France, 1963, A. Meilland; Chrysler Imperial × Charles Mallerin; darkest crimson, pointed bud opening full, 35 petals; one of the most fragrant roses yet, and not merely among moderns. Growth medium, upright; foliage glossy olive-green; mildew-prone. Under glass, this one is perfect, outdoors, the blooms need protection from sun and rain alike, so it's more an exhibition than a bedding job, and you've always got to keep that karathane spray handy. One for the specialist, beyond doubt —but at its best it can be very rewarding.

RED PLANET: Ireland, 1970, A. Dickson; parentage includes Red Devil and Brilliant; scarlet shaded crimson, paler reverse; flowers born singly and in trusses; growth upright, above average; foliage dark green, glossy. Gold Medal, Britain, 1969.

RED (Vermilion, geranium, etc.)

36 DUKE OF WINDSOR: Germany, 1968, Tantau; Spartan (fl.) ×Montezuma; light vermilion, a softer Super Star colour, with a sheen; buds high-centred and shapely, slightly smaller than average but very free; growth average height, disease-resistant except on late growth; fragrance pronounced; foliage semi-glossy dark green. Where Super Star colour is required in a lower-growing rose, the Duke is our best answer yet. Henry Edland Memorial award for fragrance and Certificate of Merit, Britain, 1968.

ISABELLE DE FRANCE: France, 1956, Mallerin; Peace ×seedling, Mme Joseph Perraud ×Opéra; high-centred buds, 25 petals, tending to open quickly, but in colour there is still nothing like it; vivid orange-scarlet, vermilion, overlaid with a dusky matt finish, so that each petal looks like velvet; average growth, free-branching, free-flowering, with none of the die-back tendencies of most of these 'hot' coloured varieties. Stands rain well but scent only slight. One of the off-beat ones that has never been replaced.

LUCY CRAMPHORN (Syn. Maryse Kriloff): France, 1960, Kriloff; Peace ×Baccara; stout, double, 40 petals, sometimes of confused centres, but equally often of exhibition form; signal-red; growth tall, upright; foliage dark green, glossy. Disease-resistant. Doesn't particularly mind rain but hates wind. Find a sheltered spot or, because of its stiff habit, there's always a chance you will find your best blooms lying broken on the stems. Said to be fragrant, but I can't detect it!

SUMMER HOLIDAY: England, 1969, Gregory; Super Star ×unnamed **37** seedling; dark vermilion, Cramphorn-type flower, very freely produced; good bedding habit, slightly above average height but well below Super Star. Like its parent, one of those that shows its presence a mile off—and one here to stay a long, long while.

SUPER STAR (syn. Tropicana): Germany, 1960, Tantau; (unnamed **3** seedling × Peace) × (unnamed seedling × Alpine Glow); intense light-bright vermilion, 35 petals, flowering as freely off side-shoots as off basal stems; above average height, about a foot taller than Ena Harkness; foliage light green and disease-resistant. Stands rain—and wind. Definitely one of the pace-setters—but is it really scented? I still don't know! Gold Medals, Bagatelle, France, Britain, Geneva, Portland, U.S., and The Hague, 1960. All-America Rose Selection, 1963.

CERISE, LIGHT RED, Etc.

FRAGRANT CLOUD (syn. Duftwolke, Nuage Parfum): Germany, **7** 1964, Tantau; unnamed seedling ×Prima Ballerina; dusky geranium-like flower, shapely, 27 petals, retaining pointed centre as it opens; very free-blooming—it just laughs at the rain! Growth strong, bushy, rather below average. Foliage bronze-green, disease-resistant. And if that's not enough, Fragrant Cloud has scent abounding. Gold Medal, Britain, 1963; International Trophy, Britain, 1964.

LEONORE DE MARCH: Spain, 1957, Camprubi; J. M. Lopez Pico × **10** Poinsettia; long-pointed buds open to statuesque carmine-scarlet flowers; growth upright, vigorous, slightly above average; very fragrant; foliage glossy green. I must admit it was the scent that first attracted me but Leonore has proved herself a lady of quiet refinement.

OPERA: France, 1949, Gaujard; La Belle Irisée × unnamed seedling; bright red-orange, shaded carmine; blooms full, well formed, refreshingly fragrant. Growth above average, inclined to be leggy. Has a 'Peace characteristic in that it resents hard pruning. Foliage light green and leathery. Keep an eye open for black spot and you'll be satisfied. Gold Medal, Britain, 1949.

REG WILLIS: Ireland, 1966, McGredy; Golden Masterpiece × Karl Herbst; deep carmine or light crimson, its flower quality is outstanding. Seldom out of bloom; 30 long, well-shaped petals. Growth sturdy, upright, and a little below average height. Foliage glossy, mid-green. One for the exhibitor but equally at home in a display bed.

10 WENDY CUSSONS: England, 1959, Gregory; Independence × Eden Rose; bloom cerise flushed scarlet, 33 petals, high-centred; exceptionally fragrant. A heavy cropper, with seldom a bad flower. Growth very vigorous, spreading, average height. Foliage dark green and glossy. One of the great British roses of my time, almost impossible to fault. If only it had been born dark red and in the age of British patents, my neighbour, Walter Gregory, must have made a fortune from it. Gold Medal and International trophy, Britain, 1959; Gold Medal, Portland, U.S., and Golden Rose of The Hague, 1964.

PINK

ANNE LETTS: England, 1954, Letts; Peace × Charles Gregory; high-pointed buds, 28 petals, opening slowly to silvery pink, a shade deeper inside; growth vigorous, thorny, slightly above average; very fragrant. Not given to disease but impatient of rain. Protect blooms from this, if necessary, and you've a great exhibition variety that also plays its part as a bedder. Foliage light green, tough and disease-resistant. Don't overdo the pruning!

ARIANNA: France, 1968, Meilland; Charlotte Armstrong × Peace × Michelle Meilland; tightly-coiled buds, opening to wide, high-centred flowers (5 in. across), of 35 petals; warm coral, splashed rosy carmine; very free-flowering; growth average height, vigorous and branching; foliage mid-green, glossy. Winner of five gold medals in Europe.

ASTREE: France, 1956, Croix; Peace × Blanche Mallerin; high-centred bloom, opening fully double; pearly pink, overshot shades of carmine and apricot; slightly above average height; highly scented; trouble free; tough, mid-green, semi-glossy foliage. One for the connoisseur but good in the garden, too.

BON SOIR: Ireland, 1969, Dickson; unnamed seedling × unnamed seedling; long-tapering buds open to full-centred flowers, apple-blossom pink in the centre shading to shell pink on the outside. One in the Ophelia–Mme Butterfly mould. Average height, vigorous growth; strongly scented; foliage mid-green and glossy. Of exhibition quality but as free-flowering as a floribunda; an undoubted hit. Gold Medal, Germany; Silver, Japan; Certificate of Merit, Britain, all 1968.

CORAL STAR: England, 1968, Robinson; parentage unknown; full flowers of 35 petals (5 in.); soft coral pink, with deeper salmon shadings; very fragrant; growth strong, rather above average height, upright; foliage mid-green, glossy.

EDEN ROSE: France, 1950, F. Meilland; Peace × Signora; ovoid bud, cupped flower, 60 petals, bright tyrian rose; growth Peace height and vigorous; strongly scented. Another equally at home in the garden or on the show bench and gloriously scented. Tough pale-green foliage. Remember its Peace parentage and spare the pruning knife!

EMBASSY: England, 1969, Sanday; parentage unknown; flower formation an exhibitor's delight, decorative in the garden, too; large (5 in.), full, 35 petals, flowers of pale gold, veined apricot and palest carmine; some fragrance; foliage dark green, glossy.

EVENSONG: Scotland, 1963, Arnot; Ena Harkness × Sutter's Gold; high-centred bloom, 25 petals, soft luminous rose-pink shading to salmon at the base; slight fragrance; growth slightly above average, vigorous and branching. Quite happy in rain. Foliage dark green, disease-resistant. Almost perfection as a bedding variety. See it just before dusk for a special thrill!

FEMINA: France, 1963, Gaujard; Fernand Arles × Mignonne; pointed buds become full, high-centred salmon-pink flowers, paling slightly on the outside; tall, vigorous grower, with flowers usually carried singly on long stems; richly fragrant, often of exhibition stature. Foliage semi-glossy, bronze-tinted medium green, needs guarding against black spot. Otherwise it's faultless.

INVITATION: United States, 1961, Swim; Charlotte Armstrong × Signora; long bud, 30 petals, salmon-pink shading to yellow at base; growth compact, branching, rather below average; very free-flowering, heavily scented with a fruity flavour. Foliage bronze green, glossy. Doesn't mind rain. A rare beauty, too often overlooked in Britain.

LADY SETON: Ireland, 1966, McGredy; Ma Perkins (fl.) × Mischief; high-centred blooms, 35 petals, medium pink, which can be of exhibition quality; growth taller than average; a winner for fragrance. Foliage mid-green, tinted bronze, and disease-resistant. Rain-resistant, too. May prove an Irish Prima Ballerina! British awards: Certificate of Merit and the Clay Cup for the best fragrant-scented rose of 1964.

40   MANUELA: Germany, 1969, Tantau, unnamed seedling × Dr A. J. Verhage; large shapely buds, opening to well-formed flowers, 27 petals; cherry pink, paling to rose pink; very fragrant. Growth average, vigorous, breaking freely from the base. Foliage dark green, glossy.

39   MISCHIEF: Ireland, 1961, McGredy; Peace × Spartan (fl.); bloom, 27 petals, large, shapely, appealing coral-salmon; growth rather above average; can be good enough for exhibition, though some blooms tend towards split centres. Foliage pale green, disease-resistant but may need watching for rust in infected areas. Still, one not to be missed! Won every award open to it—including Gold Medal and Clay Cup for fragrance, Britain, 1961.

MONIQUE: France, 1950, Paolino; Lady Sylvia × unnamed seedling; well-shaped fully double blooms, 25 petals, in the Ophelia tradition. Silvery rose pink, with salmon and carmine overlays; growth average; richly fragrant; foliage matt, light green. Freer flowering than most of the Ophelia type and a thoroughly reliable bedder.

PERCY THROWER: Belgium, 1964, Lens; La Jolla × Karl Herbst; well-formed flower, 27 petals, of silvery pink, deeper towards centre, decidedly appealing; growth average but inclined to sprawl; prune to an inward eye, as with Josephine Bruce. Slight fragrance—it is claimed. Foliage leathery, dark green. Disease and weather-resistant. A slow starter in the sales lists but now moving up, fast. Trial ground certificate, Britain.

PINK FAVOURITE: United States, 1956, Von Abrams; (Juno × seedling Georg Arends) × New Dawn (cl.); unusual breeding but this one is certainly a pace setter! Large, pointed blooms, 25 petals, exceptionally well-formed, silvery rose pink; growth just above average, strong and healthy; foliage dark green, glossy and almost perpetual. Produces a wonderful show in the garden, yet, when disbudded, probably achieves more 'best of show' blooms in the United Kingdom than any other variety. It has a pinky-apricot sport Honey Favourite (Von Abrams, 1962) identical in every way except colour.

39   PRIMA BALLERINA: Germany, 1957, Tantau; unnamed seedling × Peace; long, pointed, deep-pink buds, 20 petals; very heavily scented; growth above average—and don't try cutting it back too hard! Foliage bronze green, disease-resistant. One of the indispensables!

Pascali

Tip Top

Lilli Marlene

Oh La La
Above, in my garden

Chanelle

Dearest

Fashion

Elizabeth of Glamis

Allgold

Honeymoon

Golden Treasure

SARAH ARNOT: Scotland, 1956, Croll; Ena Harkness × Peace; full, 25 petals, high-centred rose pink; strongly scented; growth above average, branching; rain doesn't worry her and she doesn't fall easily to mildew and rust. Foliage semi-glossy and medium green. A worthwhile beauty. Gold Medal, N.R.S., 1958.

YELLOW

BATTLE OF BRITAIN: England, 1969, Gandy; Miss Ireland × Summer Sunshine; medium-sized blooms, 25 petals in floribunda-like profusion. Yellow, flushed salmon and flame on petal edges. Foliage glossy, dark green, with bronze, almost purple overtones.   19

BELLE BLONDE: France, 1955, F. Meilland; Peace × Lorraine; bright, unfading golden yellow, 25 petals; growth below average but sturdy and tough; foliage glossy, pale green. May need help against black spot but well worth any precautions.   16

DIORAMA: Holland, 1965, de Ruiter; Peace × Beauté; pointed buds, 27 petals, open to wide, well-shaped blooms; golden apricot, tinged pink; average growth, similar to Beauté; glossy-green foliage needs watching for black spot. Stands rain well; some fragrance. A variety that wasn't seen at its best in trials in Britain, at least in my opinion, but has gone ahead steadily since it came into the lists.   17

DOROTHY PEACH: England, 1958, Robinson; Lydia × Peace; flowers 37 petals, classic exhibition shape; deep-yellow flushed pink; growth sturdy but below average; highly scented; foliage semi-glossy, medium green. Protect against black spot but otherwise it is no trouble. First-class for bedding or the show bench. N.R.S. Gold Medal, 1959.

GOLD CROWN (syn. Corona de Oro; Couronne d'Or; Goldkrone): Germany, 1960, R. Kordes; Peace × Spek's Yellow; blooms long, 35 petals, opening to classic shape, borne singly on long stems; tall grower; leathery, glossy foliage, inclined to be sparse. Good for either garden purposes or exhibition. Won N.R.S. Certificate of Merit 1960 but has proved better than its Kordes 'brother', Golden Giant, which won a Gold Medal!

GRAND'MERE JENNY: France, 1950, F. Meilland; Peace × seedling Julien Potin × Sensation; long-pointed buds, 30 petals, apricot-yellow suffused pink; growth tall and upright, not so robust as Peace. Foliage glossy, medium green.   6

KABUKI: France, 1968, Meilland; (Monte Carlo × Bettina) × (Peace × Soraya); large full flowers, 5 in. across, 40 petals, deep golden yellow, holding the colour until the petals drop; tall, erect growth, as vigorous as its grandparent Peace; foliage Peace-like, dark green, glossy.

I

17 KING'S RANSOM: United States, 1961, Morey; Golden Masterpiece × Lydia; shapely blooms, 37 petals, of clear, unfading yellow. Average height, growth bushy; foliage deep green, glossy. Undoubtedly the best yellow HT bedder yet, sales increasing every year. All America winner, 1961.

LA JOLLA: United States, 1954, Swim; Charlotte Armstrong × Contrast; high-centred, 30 petals, cream flushed pink; upright grower to average height; slight fragrance; foliage light green, leathery. The first-crop flowers of this one are often the most eye-catching in the garden. The second crop, unfortunately, never seems to achieve the same subtle variations of shade. But it's a good reliable bedder and certainly one for cutting.

MARY POPPINS (syn. Lady Sunshine): Belgium, 1969, Lens; Belle Etoile × (Michelle Meilland × Tawny Gold); golden yellow pointed buds, 28 petals, opening to full, well-shaped flowers; scented too, a rare quality among yellows; growth vigorous, upright; foliage glossy, dark green.A large exhibition rose of good habit and growth.

5 PEACE (syn. Mme A. Meilland, Gioia, Gloria Dei): France, 1942, M. Meilland; (unnamed seedling × Joanna Hill) × (seedling Charles P. Kilham × Margaret McGredy); flowers, 43 petals, yellow flushed pink, are statuesque for all that it is free-flowering; habit of growth is at least 18 in. taller than the average bush rose, with branch spread accordingly. Rain-resistance good; less troubled by disease than most. Unscented but Peace is the nearest rose to perfection yet and the standard by which we have judged all its successors. It needs elbow room and hates hard pruning and in spite of a few occasionally blind shoots early on (pinch these back), it won't let you down, be you beginner or expert.

PEER GYNT: Germany, 1968, R. Kordes; parentage undisclosed; full, 36 petals, deep canary yellow, with pink flush on outer row; growth vigorous, average height but bushy; foliage light green, matt. Said to possess some fragrance. One, I think, with a big future. N.R.S. Certificate of Merit, 1967.

SPEK'S YELLOW (syn. Golden Scepter): Holland, 1947, Verschuran; Golden Rapture × unnamed seedling; bright, rich yellow, 35 petals, so free-flowering, especially towards autumn, that it needs drastic disbudding to produce a flower of normal HT size; growth rather above average; foliage leathery, glossy, dark green. Still a good bedder and useful as a decorator's rose.

30 SUTTER'S GOLD: United States, 1950, Swim; Charlotte Armstrong × Signora; yellow to light orange, veined Indian red, 32 petals, full, well-shaped, richly fragrant. Growth tall and upright, side-shoots often inclined to look spindly but will bear good blooms. Foliage glossy dark green, sometimes a victim of black spot. Still a grand rose. Certificate of Merit, Britain, 1951, after gold medals at Portland, U.S., Bagatelle, France and Geneva. All-America Award, 1950.

WESTERN SUN: Denmark, 1965, D. Poulsen; Spek's Yellow seedling × Golden Sun; deep-yellow blooms, 40 petals, of better than average colour stability; average height, upright habit; weather and disease-resistance good; foliage light green, matt. A better grower than the unreliable Golden Sun, still the best colour among the deeper yellows, and will keep its place as a bedder for this reason.

ORANGE, BUFF, etc.

ANDRE LE TROQUER: France, 1950, Mallerin; parentage undisclosed; 30 petals, yellow blending to apricot; high-pointed buds, fairly full; growth below average height but sturdy; very fragrant; foliage leathery, deep green. A variety that has not yet been bettered for the brilliance of its colour combination. Gold Medal, Britain, 1951.

ANNE WATKINS: England, 1963, Watkins; Ena Harkness ×Grand'mère Jenny; 30 petals, deep cream shading yellow, reverse apricot; high-pointed flowers, inclined to open quickly in full sun; growth below average height, sturdy, upright; foliage dark green, glossy. Reminiscent of that old favourite Comtesse Vandal, but with apricot predominating instead of pink. A much better grower than the Comtesse, though, and a rose with universal appeal for those who like the softer shades. Certificate of Merit, Britain, 1962.

BAYADERE: France, 1954, Mallerin; R.M.S. Queen Mary ×unnamed seedling; full bloom, 52 petals, of pink suffused orange, on a yellow base, a startling colour; growth above average, inclined to spread; foliage pale green, small. Needs protection against fungus diseases but worth the trouble. Some fragrance. One of my old favourites!

BEAUTE: France, 1954, Mallerin; Mme Joseph Perraud ×unnamed seedling; 27 petals, orange yellow and deep apricot; growth average, branching; spicy fragrance; foliage semi-glossy, dark green. Truly one of the classics, a rose of which I cannot see too much; still unchallenged as a bedder in this colour.

BETTINA: France, 1953, F. Meilland; Peace ×seedling Mme Joseph Perraud ×Demain; blooms full, 37 petals, but smaller than the usual HT, orange veined bronze and red; an attractive colour-combination; growth average, vigorous; foliage glossy, dark green, slightly susceptible to black spot. A distinctive rose, a decorator's delight, as yet irreplaceable.

41

42

COVER GIRL: United States, 1960, Von Abrams; Sutter's Gold × Mme Henri Guillot × seedling; orange copper gold, 32 petals; one of those colours that leap at you from yards away. Growth below average, sturdy; leaves glossy, dark green. A little fragrance—but a beauty. Mind the mildew!

DIAMOND JUBILEE: United States, 1947, Boerner; Maréchal Niel (cl.) × Feu Pernet Ducher; big, full flowers, 30 petals, buff to cream, as good for the show bench as the garden; growth above average, upright; resents hard pruning; heavily, and heavenly, scented. Note its parent, Maréchal Niel, the famous old climbing noisette rose of grandfather's day. Foliage bronze green, semi-glossy. Of quieter appearance, but a rose-man's rose.

DOREEN: England, 1951, Robinson; Lydia × McGredy's Sunset; full, 32 petals, light-orange flowers of great beauty, often with red and gold overtones. Growth below average, bushy. Petals bronze-green, semi-glossy. Needs watching for black spot and mildew, otherwise an excellent, reliable bedder.

HELEN TRAUBEL: United States, 1951, Swim; Charlotte Armstrong × Glowing Sunset; long elegant buds, 25 petals, opening to a magnificent, long-lasting petal spread; pale apricot, with pink suffusions giving a shot-silk effect. Growth above average, spreading, a graceful plant for a graceful very fragrant flower. Its only fault is a weak neck—but en masse this is all part of Helen's charms. Foliage mid-green, semi-glossy. A real delight still!

MARIGOLD: Belgium, 1955, Lens; Peace × Mme Joseph Perraud; full, 52 petals, light orange pink veined and shaded yellow, a magnificent, highly-scented bloom; growth above average, only little below Peace; foliage pale green, glossy, leathery; not prone to disease but can't stand too much rain because of its bloom size. Don't prune it too hard and you will be enchanted.

MOJAVE: United States, 1954, Swim; Charlotte Armstrong × Signora; deep apricot-orange, tinted nasturtium red; long flowers, 25 petals, inclined to open quickly but always pleasing; growth upright, above average; foliage mid-green, glossy. Gold Medals, Bagatelle, France, Geneva. All-America Award Winner, 1954.

MRS SAM McGREDY: Ireland, 1929, McGredy; seedling Donald Macdonald × Golden Emblem × unnamed seedling × The Queen Alexandra rose; coppery orange, with scarlet shades; classic form, 40 petals; growth below average, shrubby; strongly-scented; foliage coppery green, semi-glossy. I won't pretend this one doesn't need nursing but do it well and you've got one of the all-time rose wonders. There's still no colour

quite like it. Mary Wheatcroft (Robinson, 1945, Mrs Sam McGredy ×
Princess Marina) is the nearest approach though the overall effect of the
blooms is rather redder than that of the old lady herself. But Mary is a
much stronger grower!

VALENCIA: Germany, 1968, Kordes: parentage not disclosed; long
slender buds, 27 petals, of rich apricot orange; pronounced fragrance.
Kordes says Valencia is the strongest grower in this colour he has yet seen
and I'll go along with that. So this one looks like being the winner Vienna
Charm wasn't!

BICOLOURS

CHICAGO PEACE: United States, 1962, Johnson; sport from Peace;   27
identical with its magnificent parent in every way, except colour. Pink and
apricot shades, brushed over yellow, make Chicago Peace stand out as a
magnificent back-of-the-border variety. One that will last for years.

COLOUR WONDER (syn. Königin der Rosen): Germany, 1964, R.
Kordes; Perfecta ×Super Star; orange-red, brushed and tipped on yellow,
reverse of petals yellow; a rose as full as Perfecta, though the petals are
shorter, and as free as Super Star. Growth average, stout-stemmed and
very thorny. Foliage glossy, dark green. One that will go—and grow—
where Miss Ireland just dwindles.

GAIL BORDEN: Germany, 1956, Kordes; R.M.S. Queen Mary (syn.
Mev. H. A. Verschuren) ×Victoria Adelheid; large, full, 52 petals, deep
rose carmine, reverse shaded creamy yellow; growth above average,
vigorous and branching; foliage dark green, glossy. A truly handsome
flower on a handsome plant. If you want a dwarfer version, try Love Song
(syn. Liebeslied; U.S.; Fisher; 1955, Peace ×Orange Nassau). It's more
refined but not nearly so free—and it needs that extra bit of care Gail
Borden can do without. Gold Medal, Britain, 1957.

MY CHOICE: England, 1958, Le Grice; Wellworth ×Ena Harkness; full,   18
35 petals, classic shape, pink with yellow reverse, very strongly scented;
growth average, free; foliage semi-glossy, light green. Gold Medal winner,
1958, Britain, Portland, U.S., and British Clay Cup for fragrance. One
not to be missed.

PERFECTA: Germany, 1957, Kordes; Spek's Yellow ×Karl Herbst; one
of the fullest of all roses, 70 petals, its rough-looking buds open to near-
perfect flowers, cream lit with palest pink. One for the exhibitor that can
still play its part in the display garden. Growth slightly above average,
stout stems; foliage bronze green, glossy. Needs overhead protection, in all
but the best weather, to bring it to show standards but when it's there it's
great! Gold Medal, Britain, 1957; Portland, U.S., 1958.

43 PICCADILLY: Ireland, 1960, McGredy; McGredy's Yellow × Karl Herbst; 27 petals, yellow flushed orange and carmine, paler yellow on reverse, opening well whatever the weather; growth average, bushy, handsome shiny bronze-green leaves. The brightest and best bicolour for garden effect ousting its established but rather capricious rival Tzigane. My favourite, by a long way! Certificate of Merit, Britain, 1959.

37 ROSE GAUJARD: France, 1957, Gaujard; Peace × Opera; full flowers, 50 petals, white flecked pink, often deepening to plum, reverse silver; usually only one flower to a stem—but plenty of stems! Growth, tall, upright, very vigorous; foliage green, glossy. Fragrant, to boot, so you see why I, and thousands of others, rate it one of the best. Gold Medal, Britain, 1959.

41 STELLA: Germany, 1958, Tantau; Hortsmann's Jubilaumsrose (fl.) × Peace; classified as a grandiflora in the United States, but regarded as an unquestioned HT in Britain. Fully-double flowers, 36 petals, usually come in clusters but disbudding will give blooms of 'best in show' exhibition standard. Pale cream centre petals, surrounded two rings of rosy-pink ones, an attractive combination. Growth strong but rather below average height. Foliage pale green, glossy. One of the best-lookers and certainly one of the most durable in our English summers! Gold Medal, Britain, 1960.

35 TANTAU'S 6446 (as yet unnamed): Germany, 1970, Tantau; unnamed seedling × Piccadilly; dark ruby red, with silver reverse; attractive high-centred flowers, 35 petals, reflexing as they open to wide flowers, 5 in. across; growth vigorous and free to average height; foliage dark green, glossy.

WHITE, NEAR WHITE

44 MEMORIAM: United States, 1961, Von Abrams; (seedling Blanche Mallerin × Peace) × (seedling Peace × Frau Karl Druschki); white, with a faint blush tint in the centre when fully opened; full, classic shape, 60 petals; growth below average height, sturdy; foliage pale green, glossy. May need protection from disease, certainly needs protection from rain, but look after this one and you've got a great winner. Said to have been dedicated by Gordon Von Abrams as a memorial to his wife. I can only wish he'd chosen a more appealing name for a really lovely rose.

45 PASCALI: Belgium, 1963, Lens; Queen Elizabeth (fl.) × White Butterfly; white, with just a touch of palest cream; 30 petals, free-flowering and each bloom borne on a strong stem. Growth average (which means better than most whites), sturdy; leathery pale-green foliage. In my opinion, the best white yet for bedding. Tends to pink spots on the petals in bad weather but will at least open! It makes a perfect cut flower.

ROYAL HIGHNESS (syn. Königliche Hoheit): United States, 1962, **44**
Swim: Virgo ×Peace; palest lush pink under glass, usually white, with just
a pink tinge in the centre when grown in the garden; long buds, 43 petals,
open to large, exhibition-style flowers; fragrant; growth average, vigorous
and free; foliage mid-green, glossy; a more pointed flower than Memoriam
but still needs an umbrella when it rains. Markedly disease-resistant. Gold
Medals, Portland, U.S., 1960, Madrid, 1962; All-America award winner,
1963.

WHITE CHRISTMAS: United States, 1953, Swim; Sleigh Bells ×un-
named seedling; full-pointed white flowers, with plenty of body, 40 petals.
Pure white and very fragrant. Height below average but growth sturdy.
Foliage pale green, glossy. Needs protecting from the rain, if this is a
problem, rely on Pascali!

BLUE, LILAC, etc.

BLUE MOON (syn. Mainzer, Fastnacht, 'Sissi'): Germany, 1964, **24**
Tantau; unnamed seedling ×Sterling Silver; silvery lilac; full, fragrant,
growth vigorous, tall, upright; foliage glossy green, small. A better grower
than many of this colour but still needs watching for mildew and black
spot. Certificate of Merit, Britain, 1965.

COLOGNE CARNIVAL (syn. Kölner Karneval, Blue Girl): Germany, **25**
1964, R. Kordes; parentage undisclosed; silvery lilac, a shade deeper than
Blue Moon; Ophelia shaped, 40 petals; fragrant; growth vigorous, average
height; foliage glossy, dark green.

GOLDFREY WINN (syn. Millagros de Fontcuberta), Spain, 1968, Pedro **19**
Dot; parentage undisclosed; a shade paler than the first two named but
perhaps a fuller flower and certainly a stronger scent. Growth average;
foliage dark green—and healthy. Certainly a big advance on the likes of
Prélude and Sterling Silver.

INTERMEZZO: Spain, 1963, Dot; Grey Pearl ×Lila Vidri; rosy mauve,
a strong colour; full reflexed petals and plenty of flowers. Height, below
average, bushy; mid-green foliage. Of strong appeal to decorators but if
you want shape choose one of the first three above.

Floribundas

Floribundas and I seem to have grown up together. I remember, as an unwilling rose-planter of tender schoolboy years, being paid the princely sum of sixpence to embed a dozen plants for a sciatica-stricken relative. The name of one of them, doubtless imprinted in memory by countless fairytale encounters, remains with me to this day. It was called Red Riding Hood.

Now Red Riding Hood, as I remember it, was a small insignificant plant, later to produce a crop of not much more significant little red roses. One of those you would normally take one look at and forget. Or so I thought then. I now know differently. If I had a Red Riding Hood in my possession today, I would accord it, for all its lack of more obvious charms, a place of honour in my garden; indeed, in that of my nursery, as well. There I would have it, displayed for all to see, right outside my office window. For Red Riding Hood, as I was to discover in later years, was, in the country of her birth, Denmark, called Rödhätte. And Rödhätte is a gem that has made the rose-growers of this world rich, some in actual cash, many thousands more in the less definable treasures of joy and satisfaction. For little Rödhätte was virtually the mother of that ever-growing bevy of beauties we know today as the modern floribundas.

It came about in 1912, the chance result of an attempt by Dines Poulsen, in his garden at Kvistgaard near Copenhagen, to raise a new race of large-flowered roses with stamina enough to withstand the hard Scandinavian winters—just as Kordes, in Germany, had set out to master the local ice and frost by finding a hardier race of climbers. Poulsen crossed the old red polyantha poly-pom Mme Norbert Levavasseur—also known as Red Baby Rambler—with Richmond, a light-crimson scarlet American-bred, very fragrant, hybrid tea from Hill's nurseries in Indiana. Mme Norbert herself was a daughter of Crimson Rambler—that old Engineer's Rose again!

The result was Rödhätte. Poulsen knew it wasn't the ultimate answer to his quest but it was a step in the right direction. Mme Norbert Levavasseur crossed with Dorothy Perkins gave him Ellen Poulsen—and both she and Rödhätte won gold medals at Hamburg in their first year. Dines's younger brother, Svend, took over managership of the nurseries after the First World War and used the same idea; a poly-pom cross, though this time with different parents. He used Orléans Rose, reputed to be another Mme Levavasseur seedling, crossed with another crimson hybrid tea, Red Star, a semi-double. They produced Else and Kirsten Poulsen, which in 1924 were to set the whole rose world on the trail of new wonders.

Else (Joan Anderson in the United States) was a clear, deep, rose-pink semi-double, Kirsten a bright scarlet single. Both were landmarks, to be planted all over the world for their brightness and hardiness. I notice, browsing over old catalogues, that we were still listing them, as prominently as ever, even after the Second World War and they are still available from a few nurseries today, as fresh and as vigorous as ever.

Kirsten Poulsen, crossed with McGredy's red single, Vesuvius, gave Svend the crowning glory of his polyanthas, Karen Poulsen, a gold medal winner in Britain in 1933 and at Portland in the United States two years later. But it was Else that was to prove the greater influence in spreading the Red Riding Hood blood into our modern floribundas. For Kordes crossed her with a McGredy hybrid tea, Sir Basil McFarland, to produce Rosenelfe, and Rosenelfe figures in the back pedigree of many of our present-day beauties. Little Red Riding Hood really started something.

Now, why and how were they first called floribundas? There is no botanical basis for the term. The name was invented by an enterprising American nurseryman to boost his sales in a time of depression. Mr J. H. Nicholas, working for the famous Jackson and Perkins firm in New York, coined it for an advertisement boosting the new, free-flowering race of hybrid polyanthas which Jackson and Perkins had then taken up. Curiously enough, around the same time here in Britain, there was a move to get the hybrid poly-anthas incorporated into the hybrid teas. The idea was dropped in favour of the now world-recognised term floribunda, which, if not botanically correct, is at least suitably expressive. So, in my opinion, is the name grandiflora, to describe such giants of the race as Queen Elizabeth and John S. Armstrong.

Before I submit the list of my own floribunda favourites, old and new, there are two curiosities to draw to your attention. One concerns Tantau's gay little self-pink Tip Top. All over the world to-day Tip Top, raised in 1963, is being catalogued under that name and is flourishing in the sales charts. But the I.R.A.—not the Irish Republican Army this time, but the International Registration Authority for roses—steadfastly refuses to accept the name because there is still one Tip Top surviving, perhaps I should say lingering on, in a few lists issued by growers who specialise in maintaining antique roses. This one, better known under its synonym of Baby Doll, was a dwarf polyantha pom-pom, brought out in 1909 by the German Peter Lambert of Trier, who raised Frau Karl Druschki. One of its parents was the species *Rosa foetida bicolor*, the Austrian copper rose, an ancestor of our latter-day Peace.

Back to that little Red Riding Hood which began, appropriately, this story of the floribunda's rise to glory. One of its parents, as I've told you, was the damask-scented hybrid tea Richmond. Now Richmond, all over the world and especially in its native America, was for forty years or more the florists' number one choice for a red rose. Millions upon millions of plants of it were grown under glass for cutting. Naturally there came about a sizeable by-product of shedded bright-crimson petals in the nurseries and forcing houses. And with typical American business acumen, efforts were made to find a commercial outlet for this by-product of beauty. It was found among the cigarette-makers of the United States. The crimson petals of Richmond were used to become the world's first 'cork tips'—before cork itself was brought in to do the job. I wonder, is that how the brand name 'Richmond Gem' came to be invented?

46

So to my selections. For your guidance, I have picked the best from the best. As with the hybrid teas already named, I can claim to have grown most myself and have seen all the others on the nurseries of their raisers and elsewhere. I am satisfied to rely on their judgements, where necessary, as a forecast for the future.

Deliberately I have not included in this selection the strongest of the floribundas, for these, I feel, are better dealt with among the shrubs, where they, and you, will find that they enjoy a more congenial home. For an average height among floribundas I have taken Allgold, which usually grows to two and a half feet.

ALAIN: France, 1946, F. Meilland; seedling Guinée (Cl.) ×Wilhelm (sh.) ×Orange Triumph; full, scarlet-crimson flowers (2½ in. diameter), large trusses; quick to repeat; slight fragrance; growth above average; vigorous, branching; abundant mid-green foliage. An old variety now, but still an attractive one.

AMA: Germany, 1955, Kordes; Obergärtner Wiebicke ×Independence (own sister to Korona on its breeding); bright scarlet, semi-double (3 in.), large trusses, very free; growth tall, vigorous branching; foliage semi-glossy, light green. If you're tired of coping with the mildew on Frensham, this one is the answer. Trouble-free and just as capable of making a strong 5 ft. hedge.

CITY OF BELFAST: Ireland, McGredy, 1967; Evelyn Fison ×seedling Korona ×Circus; full, velvety scarlet, slightly frilled petals (2½ in.), big trusses; free-flowering; growth average height, branching, vigorous. First-class bedder, here to stay a long while. International Trophy, Britain, and N.R.S. Gold Medal, 1967.

47 EVELYN FISON (syn. Irish Wonder): Ireland, 1962, McGredy; Moulin Rouge ×Korona; brilliant velvety crimson-scarlet, full, double short-petalled flowers (2 in.); heavy trusses; growth rather below average, very sturdy, bushy; foliage bronze green, glossy, disease-resistant. An outstanding variety, seldom out of bloom, unfading in the sun, still bright and cheerful when it's raining bucketsful. I've often been cutting this one in late October—first-class blooms too. Gold Medal, Britain, 1963.

KORONA: Germany, 1953, Kordes; Obergärtner Wiebicke ×Independence; light, bright orange-scarlet; flowers 20 petals (3½ in.), sun and rain-resistant; repeats quickly; growth above average, sturdy, upright; foliage large, glossy, medium green. Don't worry about mottled plum-coloured blotches on the stems—they're natural—but watch for black spot in bad areas. Once a best-seller, it's still very popular and deservedly so. Gold Medal, Britain, 1954.

47 LILLI MARLENE: Germany, 1959, Kordes; seedling Our Princess × Rudolph Timm ×Ama; dusky scarlet-crimson, with a sheen; semi-double flowers, 25 petals (3 in.); large heads, held upright; very free; growth average height, strong, branching; foliage dark green, glossy. Just as outstanding among the darker ones as Evelyn Fison among the brighter. An impressive bedder. Certificate of Merit, Britain, 1959.

48 OH LA LA: Germany, 1957, Tantau; Fanal ×Crimson Glory (HT);

crimson-scarlet paling a little towards the centre; large ($3\frac{1}{2}$ in.), semi-double, very free; growth above average, vigorous, branching; foliage matt, medium green, large. A winner, as everyone who has seen the two beds of this variety in Queen Mary's Garden, Regent's Park, London, will surely agree.

PAPRIKA: Germany, 1958, Tantau; Marchenland × Red Favourite; bright, intense, turkey-red, shading to a curious, almost purple eye, brilliantly effective; large trusses, very free; semi-double blooms (3 in.); growth average, strong, tough leathery, dark-green foliage. In spite of more recent introductions I still have a large bed of some 150 Paprikas right outside my front door. Gold Medal, Britain, 1959; Golden Rose, The Hague, 1961.

SARABANDE: France, 1959, F. Meilland; Cocorico × Moulin Rouge; pure, startling, unfading scarlet; single flowers, 12 petals (3 in.), showing a clustered jewel of golden stamens; never out of bloom; below average height (2 ft. or under) but sturdy and branching; glossy, mid-green foliage. Another of my special favourites. Gold Medals, Bagatelle, France, Geneva, Rome, 1957; Portland, U.S., 1958. All-America award, 1960.

SCARLET QUEEN ELIZABETH: Ireland, 1963, Dickson; seedling × Korona × Queen Elizabeth; moderately full orange-scarlet blooms ($3\frac{1}{2}$ in.), not so shapely as Q.E. herself; large trusses; slightly fragrant; growth tall (about 4 ft.), very vigorous; semi-glossy dark-green foliage; an attractive, showy variety—but not a Queen Elizabeth!

VERMILION Etc.

ANNA WHEATCROFT: Germany, 1958, Tantau; Cinnabar × unnamed seedling; large (4 in.), single, soft vermilion, showing golden stamens, slightly fragrant, free-flowering in clusters; growth average, upright, sturdy; foliage dark green, glossy. Doesn't mind rain and as healthy as she is beautiful. For those who like single floribundas, as I do, this one is a must.

ARABIAN NIGHTS: Ireland, 1963, McGredy; Spartan × Beauté (HT); large ($4\frac{1}{2}$ in.), salmon-orange HT-type flowers, 25 petals, well-formed, in clusters; light scent; growth tall, vigorous, upright; foliage glossy, deep green. I can hardly call this one free flowering for a floribunda—two good flushes, with some intermittent bloom between—but it is a startling mass of colour when it is there.

DICKSON'S FLAME: Ireland, 1958, Dickson; seedling × Independence × Nymph; large ($3\frac{1}{2}$ in.), double scarlet-flame, borne freely in trusses;

slightly fragrant; growth just below average, sturdy, branching; foliage medium green, glossy. Rain-resistant and healthy. Adds a Super Star brilliance to the ranks of lower growers. Its only fault is a tendency to hang its head—largely because of the heaviness of the truss. Gold Medal and International Trophy, Britain, 1958.

60   DOROTHY WHEATCROFT: As this one is rather tall to be easily accommodated in the usual floribunda bedding groups, I include it— deservedly—in my selection of modern shrubs.

PINK

ANNA LOUISA: Holland, 1967, de Ruiter; Highlight × Valeta; per-fectly-shaped small (2 in.) shell-pink blooms, like a miniature Lady Sylvia, in clusters; dainty and attractive; quick to repeat; growth average, modera-tely vigorous, branching; foliage mid-green, glossy.

49   CHANELLE: Ireland, 1959, McGredy; Ma Perkins × seedling Fashion × Mrs William Sprott (HT); large (3 in.) semi-double, 20 petals, well-formed blooms of a subtle shade of rose pink and peach pink; slightly fragrant; very free-flowering; growth under average height, bushy and vigorous. One of the most attractive of the quieter shades; an easy colour to match up in bedding schemes. Certificate of Merit, Britain, 1958.

CITY OF LEEDS: Ireland, 1966, McGredy; Evelyn Fison × Spartan × Red Favourite; rich salmon-pink medium size, 20 petals (3 in.), HT-type blooms in well-spaced clusters; average height, sturdy branching growth; foliage mid-green, glossy. An attractive variety, in the desired category of not-too-tall growers. Gold Medal, Britain, 1965.

49   DEAREST: Ireland, 1960, Dickson; unnamed seedling × Spartan; well-formed, large (3½ in.) pale salmon-pink double blooms, 30 petals, in large clusters; growth average, bushy; foliage dark green, glossy. Can't stand too much rain but a first-class bedding variety in a good summer. Gold Medal, Britain, 1961.

50   ELIZABETH OF GLAMIS (syn. Irish Beauty): Ireland, 1965; Spartan × Highlight; large (4 in.), double, 35 petals, of soft salmon, opening flat; very fragrant; growth average, branching. Rain-resistant. Some nursery-men say this one does not take too kindly to transplanting on heavy soils— but I have not found it so. A heavenly colour and a wonderful scent. Gold Medal and fragrance cup, Britain, 1963.

FAIRLIGHT: England, 1965, Robinson; Joybells × unnamed seedling;

coppery salmon, fading to salmon with age; medium size (3 in.), semi-double flowers, 22 petals, opening flat to display anthers, good lasting quality; some fragrance; growth average, upright; foliage coppery green, glossy. An attractive, free-flowering variety, sure of a good run as a reliable bedder. Certificate of Merit, Britain, 1965.

IRISH MIST: Ireland, 1968, McGredy; Orangeade × Mischief (HT); salmon-orange, medium size (3 in.), HT-type flowers, 20 petals; borne freely in clusters; slightly fragrant; growth average height, branching; foliage dark green, small, semi-glossy. A bright attractive little newcomer that will have a lot of public appeal.

KING ARTHUR: England, 1967, Harkness; Pink Parfait × Highlight; deep salmon-pink flowers (3½ in.), 32 petals, not unlike Mischief, in clusters. Quicker to repeat with second and third crops than most of this type. Growth above average, upright; foliage glossy, dark green, dense. A beauty—but leave it on the trees, it's a disappointment when cut. Certificate of Merit, Britain, 1966.

PADDY McGREDY: Ireland, 1962, McGredy; Spartan × Tzigane (HT); large full blooms (4 in.), 32 petals, almost hybrid tea-size, deep rosy salmon, borne in clusters; slightly fragrant; weather-resistant, except for some minute red spotting on the outer petals in heavy rain. Growth below average height, bushy. Foliage pale green, leathery. When in full bloom, the flowers literally hide the petals but Paddy doesn't come again as often as we'd like, he needs a rest after that first all-out effort. His second crop is less exuberant. A good rose, needing occasional attention for black spot and rust. Gold Medal, Britain, 1961.

PERNILLE POULSEN: Denmark, 1965, Poulsen; Ma Perkins × Columbine; large (3½ in.), semi-double, 18 petals, open blooms of soft light salmon; fragrant; growth average, branching. Foliage medium green, semi-glossy. Bright and interesting bedder in a colour which must be nearing saturation point.

PINK ELIZABETH ARDEN (syn. Geisha): Germany, 1964, Tantau; parentage unknown; long pointed buds open to large (3½ in.) semi-double flowers, 24 petals of pure clear pink; large clusters, often as many as 20 flowers to a head; average height, bushy foliage, dark green, leathery, disease-resistant. As a clear, self-pink bedder, this one takes a lot of beating.

PINK PARFAIT: United States, 1960, Swim; First Love × Pinocchio; large flowers (4 in.), full-double, 23 petals, of perfect HT shape, borne in clusters; medium to light pink, with pale-yellow shadings at base; growth slightly above average, upright and branching; foliage leathery, mid-green. Altogether an elegant, attractive variety in a colour combination that I

18

find most appealing. In the opinion of many experts, the perfect HT-style floribunda. Gold Medal, Portland, U.S., 1959, Britain, 1962; All-America award winner, 1961.

46   TIP TOP: Germany, 1963, Tantau; well-formed, fragrant, medium size ($2\frac{1}{2}$ in.), salmon-pink flowers in large clusters; very free; growth below average height, branching; foliage mid-green, glossy.

YELLOW

51   ALLGOLD: England, 1956, Le Grice; ʻGoldilocks × Ellinor Le Grice (HT); medium size (3 in.), semi-double, 22 petals, slightly fragrant blooms of clear buttercup yellow, in large trusses; rain-resistant, remarkable colour-stability; growth average, a model for bedding floribundas, free and branching; foliage pale green and glossy. Le Grice has given us some great roses, but none greater than this. If only there was an Allgold in every colour! Gold Medal, Britain, 1956.

ARTHUR BELL: Ireland, 1965, McGredy; Clare Grammerstorf × Piccadilly (HT); large semi-double flowers (4 in.), 19 petals of deep yellow, red-tinged as buds; heavily perfumed. Growth slightly above average, vigorous, branching; foliage light green, glossy. An acquisition. Certificate of Merit. Britain, 1964.

52   GOLDEN TREASURE: Germany, 1965, Tantau; parentage undisclosed; deep yellow, moderately full blooms ($2\frac{1}{2}$ in.), borne free in clusters; sometimes up to 30 on a stem. Colour doesn't fade; it blooms on and on and there's no trouble with disease. Growth above average, upright; foliage dark green, glossy. If you want a yellow taller than Allgold, and as little trouble, try this one.

52   HONEYMOON (syn. Honigmond): Germany, 1960, Kordes; Clare Grammerstorf × Spek's Yellow; medium-sized, deep golden-yellow flowers (40 petals) freely produced in large clusters; growth tall, vigorous.

ORANGE, APRICOT, Etc.

COPPER POT: Ireland, 1968, Dickson; parentage undisclosed; HT-style blooms in rich orange yellow, reverse copper gold, borne in clusters—and rich profusion, scented too. Growth average height, strong and bushy. Foliage mid-green, glossy. An eye-catcher, in a colour blend we've not had before in floribundas. Unless it develops faults at present undetected or unsuspected it will become a best-seller.

Alison Wheatcroft

Charleston

Violet Carson

Iceberg

Altissimo

JOHN CHURCH: Ireland, 1964, McGredy; Ma Perkins × Red Favourite; another that looks like a miniature HT; rosette-shaped blooms ($3\frac{1}{2}$ in. when open), 47 small petals; orange salmon, free-flowering, some fragrance; growth tall, inclined to be irregular; foliage mid-green, glossy. An attractive variety.

ORANGEADE: Ireland, 1959, McGredy; Orange Sweetheart × Independence; semi-double, 12 petals, startling bright-orange blooms ($2\frac{1}{2}$ in.) in clusters. Some fragrance. Growth average, medium, inclined to be upright; foliage mid-green, semi-glossy. Needs watching for black spot and rust but still the brightest of its type. Not an easy colour to blend. Gold Medal, Britain, 1959. 53

ORANGE SENSATION: Holland, 1961, de Ruiter; parentage undisclosed; orange vermilion, full ($2\frac{1}{2}$ in.), 24 petals; good clusters; fragrant; considerable rain-resistance; growth vigorous, average height, branching; foliage medium green, matt. Needs watching for disease but worth every trouble. A magnificent cut-flower under artificial light. Gold Medal, Britain, 1961.

ORANGE SILK: Ireland, 1968, McGredy; Orangeade × seedling Ma Perkins × Independence; orange vermilion, large (4 in.), full, 25 petals, flowers of HT shape, borne in clusters, fewer to the stem than Orange Sensation. Growth average height, branching, vigorous; foliage dark green, glossy. It could be called a brighter, tidier, more uniform Orange Sensation but there's still room for both varieties. 53

SIR LANCELOT: England, 1967, Harkness; Vera Dalton × Woburn Abbey; unusual apricot-yellow, clear self-colour, tending to deepen in cooler weather; blooms semi-double ($3\frac{1}{2}$ in. across), 18 petals, borne in well-spaced clusters, opening to show stamens; growth average, vigorous and branching; small light-green matt foliage. One of Jack Harkness's first products since he began raising . . . and one that's here for a long stay.

WOBURN ABBEY: England, 1962, Sidey and Cobley; Masquerade × Fashion; large ($3\frac{1}{2}$ in.), double, 25 petals, orange, tinted salmon-orange, cupped flowers in clusters. Some fragrance. Growth average, branching; foliage dark green, leathery. Needs watching for mildew but is proving tougher than it first looked.

ZAMBRA: France, 1961, M. L. Meilland; (seedling Goldilocks × Fashion) × (seedling Goldilocks × Fashion). Real in-breeding this and a really bright product. Semi-double, 12 petals ($2\frac{1}{2}$ in.), flowers of nasturtium-orange, bright yellow reverse, in clusters up to 15 in. across. Growth below average 54

K

height, branching; foliage glossy, light green. Needs watching for mildew and will sulk if she's neglected. But give her due care and attention and she's a winner! Gold Medals, Bagatelle, (France) Rome, 1961.

BICOLOURS

55   ALISON WHEATCROFT: England, 1959, Wheatcroft Bros.; sport from Circus (Fandango, HT × Pinocchio); double blooms (3 in.), 25 petals, of apricot flushed orange; Masquerade-type but stable colouring, gay without being strident. Scented, always in bloom, laughing at weather and viruses alike. Growth average, vigorous, branching; foliage semi-glossy, dark green. One of my favourites and not just because it's one of the family. A wonderful bedder.

56   CHARLESTON: France, 1963, A. Meilland; Masquerade × seedling Radar (HT) × Caprice (HT); scarlet and gold ($3\frac{1}{2}$ in.), 20 petals, semi-double, large clusters; a more refined Masquerade, much easier to manage in a bed. Growth average, sturdy, branching; foliage dark green, glossy. Unmatched so far but watch out for black spot.

DAILY SKETCH: Ireland, 1961, McGredy; Ma Perkins × Grand Gala (HT); large, double ($3\frac{1}{2}$ in.), 40 petals, well-formed HT-shaped flowers, pink on silver reverse, in well-spaced clusters; fragrant, free-flowering, not unlike a smaller, paler Rose Gaujard. Growth above average, upright, vigorous; foliage dark green, glossy. Gold Medal, Britain, 1960.

REDGOLD: Ireland, 1967, Dickson; (seedling Karl Herbst × Masquerade) × (seedling Faust × Piccadilly); deep gold, edged and flushed cherry red; blooms medium sized (3 in.), full HT-type in clusters. Growth medium height, upright; foliage semi-glossy, small, medium green. Take just one bloom and it looks nothing but taken en masse the effect is startling. Certificate of Merit, Britain, 1966.

SHEPHERDESS: England, 1967, Mattock; Allgold × Peace (HT); semi-double (3 in.), yellow, veined and painted salmon, 15 petals; some fragrance. Growth average height, vigorous, branching. Foliage bronze-tinted dark green. Refined, restrained, consistent—a little beauty that will go a long way.

SHEPHERD'S DELIGHT: Ireland, 1956, Dickson; Masquerade seedling × Joanna Hill (HT); blooms (3 in.), semi-double, 15 petals, flame, orange and yellow—the Masquerade colours, only unchanging. Large trusses, fragrant. Growth tall and branching. Foliage dark green, semi-glossy. Guard against black spot but a fine variety for the back of the border; a big improvement on Masquerade itself. Gold Medal, Britain, 1958.

TRIO: Ireland, 1966, Dickson; parentage undisclosed; clear gold and red in early stages, changing to gold and deep rose; HT-shaped large (4 in.) flowers, 20 petals, held firm and high on long stems. Growth rather above average, upright; foliage dark green, glossy. First-rate for cutting—and shines just as well in the garden. A most attractive young lady.

VIOLET CARSON: Ireland, 1963, McGredy; Mme Leon Cuny (HT) × Spartan; full-double (3 in.), 35 petals, classic-shaped HT-type flowers in well-spaced, large clusters; delicate salmon, reverse silvery, a delightful combination; fragrant. Growth slightly below average height, upright, bushy; foliage bronze green, glossy. One of the real gems I'll always keep in my collection. 56

WHITE

ICEBERG (syn. Schneewittchen; Fée des Neiges): Germany, 1958, R. Kordes; Robin Hood (h. musk) × Virgo (HT); flowers large (4 in.), moderately full, 24 petals, opening flat; pink tinged in bud, pure white later; slight fragrance; growth tall (4 to 5 ft.), slender, but hardy and very vigorous; foliage light green, glossy. One of the real greats among floribundas; you can use it in the shrubbery, for a hedge, or as a tall bedder; anywhere it's outstanding for its grace. Gold Medal, Britain, 1958. 57

ICE WHITE: Ireland, 1966, McGredy; Mme Leon Cuny (HT) × seedling Orange Sweetheart × Tantau's Triumph; creamy-white, moderately full, 20 petals, slightly fragrant; lower grower than Iceberg, robust and branching; foliage mid-green, semi-glossy. Won't disgrace the older variety but there's room enough for both.

LILAC, BLUE, etc.

LAKE COMO: England, 1968, Harkness; Lilac Charm × Sterling Silver (HT); soft lilac, showing stamens nestling on top of reflexed petals in the fully open bloom; neat cluster; 20 petals; some fragrance; growth moderate, bushy, healthy; foliage dark green. Attractive, wants the weather.

LAVENDER LASSIE: see Shrub Roses.

LILAC CHARM: England, 1961, Le Grice; parentage undisclosed; single, 12 petals, pale lilac mauve, a wonderful sight with its golden stamens and deep contrasting ruby-red filaments. Unfortunately, this fleeting moment of glory is rarely seen out of doors. Growth below average (about 18 in.), bushy; foliage dark green, leathery. I don't suggest you try it as a bedder but one or two plants should provide material to delight the lady of the house in her decorations. 24

Climbers

If you have ever balanced atop a twelve-foot ladder, its feet sinking in soil at the base of a wall while you tried, in a cold, blustery wind to cope with pruning a rampant Albertine, you will have some sympathy for the gardeners of Burma. They may not have our chill blasts but they do have a native climber—*Rosa gigantea*, we call it —that grows to fifty feet, and sometimes eighty feet or more. Its main stems are as thick as a man's arm. Its lateral branches sweep off into massive thirty-foot lengths and they, in turn, give rise to 'twigs' of six foot or more! Truly, this is the giant of the rose world and I wonder what those Burmese Percy Throwers choose to under-plant it with. Teak trees?

Now *Rosa gigantea* can be induced to begin to grow in a few favoured spots in Britain. But it is not hardy and seldom reaches a length of more than twelve feet—less than our Albertines and New Dawns—before even a moderate frost cuts it dead. *Gigantea* has, however, been used by a few breeders, notably Paul Nabonnand, on the Mediterranean coast of France, and Alister Clark, in Australia, to give us hybrids that at least stand some chance of survival here. Clark's Lorraine Lee, remarkably persistent with its blooms of fragrant terra-cotta pink, and his Kitty Kininmonth, raised two years earlier (in 1922), with its mass of carmine-rose clusters, are notably hardier than the type and, with shelter against winds and cutting frosts, both can be induced to flourish here out-doors. Both, incidentally, are amazingly disease-free.

But it is of the tallest climber in Britain that I want to tell you now. It grows indoors, in a greenhouse the size of the average surburban house's back garden. It is a *gigantea* hybrid called La Follette, raised in the early 1900s—no one now knows the exact date—by an English gardener called Busby, working on the French Riviera estate at Cannes of Lord Brougham and Vaux. Bubsy, good and faithful servant that he was, refused to tell anyone what other rose he had employed to cross with his *gigantea* species to produce La Follette—the name means 'the wanton one'—but it is thought to have been a tea rose. Anyway a Captain George Warne, of Roquebrune, also in the South of France, is known to have obtained a plant of La Follette from the veteran Busby in 1924; and from there the wanton one made her way to England.

The specimen of which I write came here as a cutting some thirty-five years ago, to be rooted in a conservatory at Southill Park, Bedfordshire, the property of the Whitbread family. (I am grateful to Mr. S. C. Whitbread for his help in finding the pictures.) There it stands today; so rampant, so full of life, that it seems to be bursting out of its protective surroundings. Its main stems rise sheer out of the ground for fifteen feet. Then it really begins to grow out—like a grapevine. It flings its branches fifty feet in length; across the conservatory for thirty feet or more and all at an altitude of almost twenty feet above soil level! Careful records are kept of the number of flowers it produces each year—from Christmas to March—and the average, I am told, is 2,000. Two thousand first-class blooms from one plant . . . a rose-man's dream! But pruning must be a rose-man's nightmare. It takes, so they say, almost a week, just to do this one plant! So I urge you to think of that next time you are cutting back those far more restrained climbers in the back garden, however awe inspiring their tangle of shoots and prickles may seem to you!

Handling the climbers seems to me to cause the biggest of all rose worries to amateur gardeners, whenever pruning time comes round. 'What is the difference between a climber and a rambler: how can I tell them apart and how do I prune them?' Professionals through the ages must have been asked that question more than any other by the anxious novices. And, for my part, I know I have been asked it on every single lecture tour I have made across the

La Follette, showing Mr. Malcolm, the Southill gardener, tying in new growth, and its flowers twenty feet above ground level. (*Harkness Roses, Hitchin*)

world from Altrincham to Australia! The answer is basically simple and I can do not better than quote the descriptions given in the Royal National Rose Society's official type classification: 'Ramblers are mostly hybrids of *R. wichuraiana* or *R. multiflora*, of vigorous but lax growth, bearing small flowers in clusters. Climbers are of stiffer vigorous growth, and with larger flowers.'

Now I feel is the time to emphasise what has always been a sore point with me. I am always distressed, after I have sold someone a collection of roses, to be told, years later: 'Oh they have done very well but I have lost the names.' Losing the variety names suggests to me a carelessness I can hardly identify with any true rose lover. Even if you don't retain the labels, do, I urge you, keep a record, even down to the siting in the bed, of varieties you have planted—it makes the garden so much more interesting. But in no class of roses is this more important than with climbers. With names available, one glance at a catalogue, if you're still not sure, will tell you to what group your climber belongs, and the appropriate pruning treatment can be applied immediately. The problem of whether it is a climber or a rambler may still arise, of course, over plants that were in the garden before you arrived. This question is mentioned in the Introduction, but there is more to be said about it.

The Rose Society's description is an accurate guide. But there is one other clue I try to give my questioners if they are still in doubt. I ask them: 'Do you know Dorothy Perkins?' Now Dorothy Perkins is that small, pale green-leaved climber of the many floppy canes, which for two weeks a year is covered in a mass of small bright-pink blossoms but which, for most of the rest of the season, seems to cloak itself in a furry-white overcoat of mildew. It came out in 1901, raised by the American firm of Jackson and Perkins, and was named Dorothy after the then small grand-daughter of Dr Perkins. Poor girl! Her namesake was a martyr to disease. It must have gone into every garden in the world in the first half of this century, patiently suffering its seemingly inevitable coating of mildew before experiencing its next moment of fleeting glory in a month's time. Purely for the reward of that two week's bloom, everyone grew Dorothy Perkins—and many still do. That's why I ask if you know it?

Now if that unidentified climber of yours *is* like Dorothy, freely-branching and whippy-stemmed, you can be ninety-five per cent sure it's a wichuraiana-type rambler, as she is. And for these the pruning is simple, albeit time-devouring and flesh-gashing. After flowering, untie all the shoots from the supporting arch, fence or wall, cut out those that have borne flowers and re-tie the remainder into place, so that they form the basis of next year's display. If, for any reason, there should be a shortage of new basal canes, a few of the older ones may be retained to help out—but never for longer than one year. All the time the plant is growing, the young shoots must be carefully tied in, to prevent wind damage or any of the other hazards fleshy young shoots are subject to, until permanent tieing-in time arrives.

All this involves constant work and, if I know my gardeners, quite a few edgy tempers. A mass of effort for, let's face it, only a brief period of reward. That is why raisers set out to find for us the remontant, or perpetual flowering, climbers. Roses that would go on giving us a fair return, all through the season, for our labour of love. Not only are these freer blooming; their flower production requires much less effort. Simply cut out the old dead, dying or diseased wood, or any that is unripe, just tip the laterals—the side-shoots—be sure the branches are firmly secured to their supports—and get ready to greet the new season's flowers. Perpetual flowered climbers—and most of those we supply today come into that category—are best pruned in early spring.

Climbing sports of hybrid teas—of which, incidentally, there must have been almost 350 recorded so far—need similar treatment. That temperamental sulphur-yellow single rose, Mermaid, uncertain but capable of so much magnificence, needs very little pruning at all. Just get out any dead or unripe wood. And you won't be incited to do a lot more in any case, for this one, in all but the most severe frosts, retains its foliage throughout the year. A rose evergreen.

Whether your garden be large or small, a selection of climbers is essential to give it the dimension of height it needs for overall beauty. Don't buy any old climber just to cover up a bare space or unsightly wall. Choose them carefully, treat them well and the lasting reward of infinite pleasure will be yours. From the select list

23

Golden Showers climbing a fence.

One of the stronger-growing species roses—*R. Banksiae*—used as a climber. A superb adornment to a splendid old house.

which follows I think you will find just the variety to suit every purpose. Most are good all-rounders; where one is better adapted for a particular purpose, I have not hesitated to say so.

In many varieties, notably Crimson Glory, the climbing sports show no sign, at present, of the vegetative degeneration—advancing age—now affecting their parent bush types. In many, too— Crimson Glory, Spek's Yellow, Shot Silk, Mrs Sam McGredy— the individual blooms are bigger and often better coloured than those usually obtained from the varietal norm.

One thought more: I have never gone along with the old pundits who argued that no climbing sport should ever be hard pruned or it would revert to its bush type. All the sports in my list have shown fixed climbing characteristics and if, for any reason such as frosting or disease, you should have to cut back their stems hard, you need have no fear that you will be left with a bush plant, instead of the climber intended. In all my experience I have never seen it happen. But prune those long ripe shoots as little as you can, that's sense. And train as many as you are able laterally—in a fan shape. That's the way to get the lower eyes to break and to ensure more flowers.

ALTISSIMO: France, 1967, Delbard-Chabert; parentage undisclosed; **58**
large-flowered single (4 in.), shining deep red with crimson overtones,
attractive deep golden-yellow stamens, like a red Mermaid; growth
vigorous, sturdy, to above 12 ft.; foliage matt, medium green. A highly
decorative new variety, seemingly trouble-free. Certificate of Merit,
Britain, 1965.

CASINO (syn. Gerbe d'Or): Ireland, 1963, McGredy; Coral Dawn × **21**
Buccaneer (HT); large (3½ in.), full, 42 petals, soft yellow flowers, shapely
HT-type, paling slightly with age; usually carried in small trusses; some
perfume; quick to repeat. Growth vigorous to 10 ft. Ideal for pillars.
Foliage large, glossy, dark green, disease-free. Sam McGredy, the raiser,
says this one replaces climbing McGredy's Yellow—and I agree. A notable
acquisition. Gold Medal, Britain, 1963—the first of the remontants to be
so honoured.

DANSE DU FEU (syn. Spectacular): France, 1953, Mallerin; Paul's **22**
Scarlet Climber × *R. multiflora* seedling; medium-sized double flowers, 33
petals, in clusters, opening flat; brilliant orange scarlet, some fragrance.
Growth vigorous and branching to 12 ft. Because of its freedom, it is easier
handled, in my opinion, on a wall or fence than as a pillar rose. Abundant
recurrent bloom. Foliage mid-green, glossy, disease-resistant. Certain to
remain a best-seller for years.

DORTMUND: Germany, 1955, Kordes; unnamed seedling × *R. kordesii*;
large (4½ in.) single flowers, dark red with white eye, borne freely in heavily-
loaded clusters; sometimes as many as 20 flowers to the truss. Very free,
blooming almost continuously. Some scent. Growth strong, vigorous to
10 ft. Foliage dark green, glossy. Weather and disease-resistant. Best as a
pillar but capable of making a large specimen bush for use in the shrubbery.
One of the indispensables.

GOLDEN SHOWERS: United States; 1957, Lammerts; Charlotte
Armstrong (HT) × Capt. Thomas; long pointed daffodil-yellow buds in
clusters opening to large (4 in.) double flowers, 30 petals, becoming flat;
quick to recur; good weather-resistance. Growth strong, upright to 10 ft.
Foliage pale green, glossy. Perfect as a pillar or shrub. Gold Medal,
Portland, U.S., 1957; All-America award, 1957.

HAMBURGER PHOENIX: Germany, 1954, Kordes; *R. kordesii* × seedling; long pointed buds open to full 25 petals (3 in.), red rich flowers in
clusters; slightly fragrant. Profuse repeated bloom. Growth strong, vigorous
to 15 ft., freely branching. Foliage dark green, glossy. Suitable for walls,

fences or pillars. An attractive, trouble-free variety, extremely weather-resistant, and, like most *kordesii* types, extremely hardy.

HANDEL: Ireland, 1965, McGredy; Columbine (fl.) ×Heidelberg (shrub); large (3½ in.), double, 22 petals, HT-type blooms of cream edged pink, borne in clusters. Quick repeat blooms. Growth vigorous, upright to 8 ft. Foliage olive green, glossy. Ideal pillar habit—a little beauty now in world-wide demand. Resistant to rain in spite of its delicate looks.

21 MAIGOLD: Germany, 1953, Kordes; Poulsen's Pink (fl.) ×Frühlingstag (*H. spinosissima*); pointed golden-yellow buds opening to large (3½ in.), semi-double bronze-yellow blooms of 14 petals, revealing stamens. Consistent repeat flowering; very fragrant. Growth very vigorous, branching—and very thorny—to 10 ft. or more. Foliage pale green, semi-glossy. Altogether a most attractive variety for walls, fences, pillars, even in the shrubbery. Where Mermaid won't grow, try this one. You won't be disappointed.

MEG: England, 1954, Gosset; officially a climbing HT; parentage believed Paul's Lemon Pillar ×Mme Butterfly (HT); large (5 in. across), single, 10 petals, flowers of soft salmon apricot with peach shadings, surrounding a cluster of red-tipped stamens. Caught just right, an unforgettable beauty. Repeats consistently. Appreciable fragrance. Growth very vigorous, branching. Ideal for walls, fences—or even climbing into old tree stumps. If you have to tie it in anywhere, don't delay this operation unduly, Meg's stems, as they age, get tough and almost intractable. Foliage bronze green, glossy. For those who like quiet beauty in their roses, this is one not to be missed. Gold Medal, Britain, 1954.

23 MERMAID: England, Paul 1918; *R. bracteata* ×unnamed double yellow tea rose; strictly a hybrid *bracteata*—and a classic climber. Large (up to 6 in.) pale sulphur yellow single flowers, showing a ring of amber stamens; almost sculptured beauty; flowers sometimes singly, sometimes in small clusters. Repeats consistently. Growth very vigorous, possibly up to 25ft.; foliage pale green, glossy. A dream-girl—but one warning. Mermaid is temperamental, can't stand cold and is usually slow to establish herself on transplanting. On the nursery she is usually propagated in pots; no 'usual treatment' for her! Forgive her all her faults; she's a wonderful rose if she likes you enough to settle down. Gold Medal, Britain, 1917.

MORNING JEWEL: Scotland, 1968, Cocker; New Dawn ×Red Dandy (fl.); glowing rich pink, fully double flowers (3½ in.), produced freely from growing tips as well as laterals. Constantly in bloom; markedly fragrant and delightful and long-lasting for cutting. Growth to about 12 ft., similar to New Dawn. Foliage mid-green, glossy. An aptly-named jewel—morning, afternoon or evening!

PARKDIREKTOR RIGGERS: Germany, 1957, Kordes; *R. kordesii* ×
Our Princess (fl.); pointed buds opening to medium-sized (3 in.) semi-
double flowers, 15 petals, in large clusters; as many as 50 flowers to a
cluster is not uncommon; sparkling velvety crimson, slightly fragrant; good
repeat flowering. Growth very vigorous, up to 15 ft., branching. Foliage
dark green, glossy. Ideal for walls or fences but guard against mildew on
the new shoots if it is grown against a wall. And because of its colour it looks
better against a white wall than a red brick one.

PINK PERPETUE: England, 1965, Gregory; Danse du Feu × New
Dawn; full, 32 petals (3½ in.), semi-globular bright rose-pink flowers in
clusters; very free recurrent blooming; markedly fragrant. Growth vigorous,
branching to 10 ft.; foliage pale green, matt. Hardly a graceful beauty but
a warming splash of colour on any wall or fence. Rather too freely-
branching, with stems too thick to be an ideal pillar rose in my opinion but
for hardiness and honest effort one hard to beat. Certificate of Merit,
Britain, 1954.

ROSY MANTLE: Scotland, 1968, Cocker; New Dawn × Prima Ballerina
(HT); large fully-double, HT-shaped flowers in warm rosy pink. Heavy
crops in summer and autumn, intermittent between. Strongly fragrant;
lasts well when cut. Growth strong, vigorous to 8 ft. A welcome addition.

ROYAL GOLD: United States, 1957, Morey; (cl.) Goldilocks × Lydia
(HT); full, 36 petals (4 in.), deep yellow flowers of perfect HT-shape; the
deepest yellow of all climbers. Repeats well. Growth moderately vigorous
to 10 ft. Foliage mid-green, glossy. Needs a reasonably sheltered site and
good growing conditions; then it's a gem. May suffer from winter die-back
in colder winters but otherwise healthy. At its best a grand flower. A pillar
rose for preference.

SOLDIER BOY: England, 1953, Le Grice; unnamed seedling × Guinée;
large (5 in.), single, velvety scarlet, with prominent golden anthers. Very
heavy first flowering, with some bloom until another showy autumn crop.
Growth very vigorous, to 12 ft., freely-branching. Foliage light green,
leathery. For those who like singles, a real beauty.

SWEET SULTAN: England, 1953, Eacott; Independence (fl.) × Honour
Bright; another large crimson single, 5 petals (5 in. across), with attractive
maroon shadings. Repeats well. Growth strong, branching, to 9 ft. Dark
green, leathery foliage which—unusual feature—takes on typical autumn
tints at the season's end. An attractive, interesting variety that raises the
question: will the next step be raising rose for their decorative foliage as
well as flowers?

THE NEW DAWN: United States, 1930, Somerset Rose Nurseries; recurrent-blooming sport of hybrid wichuraiana Dr Van Fleet; full, 27 petals, cameo-pink flowers ($3\frac{1}{2}$ in.), fading to flesh white with age, in large well-spaced clusters; refreshingly fragrant. Unlike its once-a-year parent, New Dawn (patented No. 1 in the States), is seldom out of bloom. Growth very vigorous, like a typical rambler, to 25 ft. Glossy, pale-green foliage. New Dawn is too strong for a pillar rose; give her her head over fences, walls, old trees or down banks and you've got a winner that will last for years. One word of warning: she flowers on old wood, so prune sparingly.

RAMBLER ROSES

23 ALBERTINE: France, 1921, Barbier; *R. wichuraiana* × Mrs A. R. Waddell (HT); salmon buds opening to full, coppery-orange flowers, 25 petals ($3\frac{1}{2}$ in.). Fruity fragrance. Growth very vigorous, branching, to 20 ft. Foliage bronze green, glossy, small. One crop of flowers only but this is long lasting, little affected by the weather, and so profuse that the whole plant seems to be buried under a floral avalanche. Too strong for the average pillar, but blissfully happy anywhere else. For really tricky situations, this is the one to try. If Albertine fails, the only other climber I can recommend is ivy!

ROSE MARIE VIAUD (syn. Amethyst); France, 1924, Igoult; fixed colour sport from Veilchenbläu (see below); rich, true amethyst flowers in huge clusters. Can also be grown as a large spreading bush in the shrubbery. Unlike the parent variety—and most other ramblers—this colour sport seems mildew-free. Don't ask me why!

VEILCHENBLAU (syn. Violet Blue): Germany, 1909, Schmidt; Crimson Rambler × unnamed seedling; small ($1\frac{1}{2}$ in.), semi-double, cupped, flowers of distinct deep violet, with white eye—the truest blue I have yet seen in any rose. Heavily-laden clusters; very free-flowering (one heavy crop in July). Distinct fragrance. Growth very vigorous; many canes stretching to 15 ft. or more. Foliage large, light green, glossy. Not only has it historical value, its a gay, distinct beauty in its own right, still holding its own with the charmers of today.

CLIMBING HT SPORTS

All climbing HT sports are identical with the bush varieties from which they have sprung, in every way except growth. In any garden where climbers can be featured, these, I think, are worth their place. Dates of introduction given are those, of course, of the climbing sport:

Cl. CAROLINE TESTOUT: France, 1901, Chauvry.
Cl. CRIMSON GLORY: United States, 1946, Jackson & Perkins; another sport originated in South Africa.
Cl. ENA HARKNESS: England, 1954, Murrell.
Cl. JOSEPHINE BRUCE: England, 1960, Bees.
Cl. LADY SYLVIA: England, 1933, Stevens; strong grower, plant needs to get really well-established before it flowers in full glory.
Cl. MRS SAM McGREDY: Holland, 1937, Buisman; also sported in U.S. (Somerset Rose Co., 1940).
Cl. SHOT SILK: Australia, 1931, G. Knight; also England, 1937, Prince.
Cl. SPEK'S YELLOW: 1956, Walters, U.S.A.
Cl. SUPER STAR: 1968, sported in England, on the Continent and in the United States, all in the same year.

Shrubs

Fantin Latour. Cardinal de Richelieu. Felicité et Perpetué. Mme Pierre Oger. Nuits de Young. The names themselves are redolent of crinolines and parasols; of warm summer afternoons in the gracious, spacious days of a bygone age. Personally, I can never look upon any display of the old-fashioned shrub roses, with all their intriguing, scented beauty, without my mind wandering back across the years.

Entering a garden of shrub roses is to me like visiting an ancestral home, since so many of our modern charmers, especially among the hybrid teas, owe their origins to roses that flourished under the loving care of generations of gardeners long gone but never forgotten.

A shrub rose garden is for memories and relaxation. I realise that, with land values soaring like moon-bound rocket ships, gardens everywhere are inevitably getting smaller. But even in the mini-plots that surround so many homes today, space can still be found for the occasional shrub rose, even if only as a replacement for the ever-hungry laurels or the temperamental lilac in the corner. Ideally, if space permits, there should be a shrub rose corner as part of every rose garden; a grove of nostalgic delights for comparatively little effort.

Nor is it essential today that our choice of occupants should be restricted to the varieties great-great grandfather tended—officially an 'old shrub rose' is one introduced before 1900—for though the strongest emphasis has been on the development of new hybrid teas and floribundas, new shrub varieties have not been entirely forgotten by the today's hybridists. Indeed, for continuity of flowering, I would recommend anyone constructing a new shrub rose garden today to stock at least half of it with modern introductions. The choice is wide. All the colours of the rose's paintbox are available.

Many of the most elegant of our modern, more restrained, climbers make admirable shrub roses, left to grow unfettered, unrestrained by archways or wall supports. For instance, the charming, soft coral-pink perpetual-flowering climber Aloha is conventionally used as a pillar rose, but in my opinion it is far better treated as a free-growing shrub. So is the attractive Golden Showers and that bronze-yellow highly-scented startler, Maigold. **21** Officially, this one is listed as a non-recurrent bloomer but my own plants usually seem to bear a second crop, less generous it is true than their July offerings but welcome none the less.

One of the most beautiful sights of early summer is the unfolding of those giant butterflies of flowers tumbling from the wide-flung wings of the hybrid *spinosissimas* Frühlingsgold and her sister **61, 62** Frühlingsmorgen; the former in palest gold, Frühlingsmorgen with a radiant blush of pink on her basic yellow. Aptly are these two named Spring Gold and Spring Morning. Both are post-war introductions, brought out by Kordes when he was striving to find climbers hardy enough to stand the rigours of the North German winter. Frühlingsgold offers the added bonus of a glorious scent while her five-year younger sister gives a second crop of flowers in the autumn. Also in the autumn, Nevada is a dazzling giant, snow-capped like the Sierras themselves. If my old friend Pedro Dot had never given us any other rose than this, he would still have been remembered.

I would find a place in any shrub garden for McGredy's Uncle Walter, that bright crimson, of almost perfect shape and wanton profusion of bloom, that is, alas, too tall for a normal bedding rose. Another of McGredy's hybrid teas, the deep-yellow Bossa Nova, had also to be re-classified as a shrub rose for the same reason.

At the other end of the scale, I can commend one that seems to

L

An attractive arrangement
of shrub roses.

have dwindled! Cocktail is a charming climber in its native Southern France. Here in Britain, and from what I have seen of it in America, it can scarcely be called rampant and, in any case, its slender shoots are often cut back by frost. But as a shrub it is still a desirable beauty, with its spectacular offerings of carmine and gold, set like gem stones around an open cluster of golden anthers. First Choice, with its five-inch single flowers of orange scarlet with yellow-ringed hearts, is a home-raised beauty from Norfolk that I like.

To bring colour to a shrub garden throughout the season, these modern introductions are indispensible. Any of the stronger-growing hybrid teas or floribundas—Peace, Eden Rose, Chicago Peace, Dame du Coeur, Dorothy Wheatcroft, Fred Loads, Iceberg, Chinatown, to name only a few—also make excellent specimen trees. Just prune them lightly and let them grow.

One of the great advantages of shrub roses, so far as a busy gardener is concerned, is that they do not need the same attention demanded by the hybrid teas and floribundas displayed as bedders. They make, in fact, even less demands on time than the upkeep of an uninspiring privet hedge kept presentably shorn. Annual pruning is reduced to a mere cutting out of dead stems and the elimination of any awkwardly-sited canes developing among the new shoots. The disease-resistance of most shrub roses is high.

Certainly among the old shrub roses there is none of that unfortunate tendency to lose vigour through repeated propagation—the life-sapping factor known as vegatative degeneration which I have already mentioned and which is bringing an end of some hybrid tea varieties, even of some post-war introductions. Some of the old shrub species still growing in our gardens today are known to have been in cultivation since the days of the Romans.

How long can a rose tree live? The average 'working age' of a modern hybrid tea or floribunda variety is around ten or fifteen years. But the oldest known living rose plant in the world is a specimen of the species *Rosa canina*—the common dog rose of our hedges—which, according to authenticated records, has been in existence more than five hundred years and may be even twice that age. This rose is a plant growing among the cloisters of Heidelsheim Cathedral, in Germany. Archives record its existence there for at least five centuries—and the legend, which may be true, is that it was originally planted one thousand years ago by the Emperor Charlemagne. Plant biologists from all over the world have examined this plant but there are no age-revealing cambium rings, such as there are in a forest tree, to guide them in their calculations. Some may doubt if it is as much as ten centuries old, though no one has yet said categorically that it cannot be. To German rose-growers the Rose of Heidelsheim is now almost a national shrine. Way back in 1884 the plant was seen to be dwindling through age and lack of fertile soil. A life-saving operation was carried out by a small group of local enthusiasts. Rubbish of centuries was cleared from the roots—rubble almost four feet deep. New loam was brought in to replace it. A watering system was installed, specially for that one historic plant. By 1944 it was thirty-two feet high. This tree that was flourishing long before the Great Fire of London, was itself almost burned to the ground when fire destroyed its sheltering cathedral during an air raid the following spring. Happily the rootstock was unaffected. Now its limbs stretch out more than thirty feet again. And I tell you its story merely to illustrate the longevity of the species, and to show how they can bear any treatment from a neglectful gardener.

If they could talk, these species roses would have rare tales of history to tell. A variety of *Rosa gallica*, said to have been brought to England from France by a son of our first King Edward, was the red rose adopted by the House of Lancaster as their symbol in the Wars of the Roses. The rival white rose of York was, according to plant historians, undoubtedly *Rosa alba*, the rose which, according to the elder Pliny, the eminent Roman naturalist, gave England its title of Albion. It was a single rose then. Now it is the double forms, botanically known as *Rosa alba plena*, which are mostly in cultivation today and, somewhat ironically you may think, the finest variety of all the *albas* is not a white rose at all but a soft delicate pink, Maiden's Blush, which originated at Kew in 1797.

The so-called York and Lancaster rose is sometimes said to symbolise the mediaeval reunion of the two warring houses because it bears white and deep-pink (not red) flowers on the same stem. It is a variety of *Rosa damascena*, the Damask Rose. The earliest-known reference to it dates from 1550, sixty-six years after the Wars of the Roses ended, and it was unknown in this country until the late 1600s. So the reunion story, romantic though it may be, is clearly fable.

Damask roses themselves are known to have been in cultivation in Europe for at least four thousand years. Wall paintings existing at the ancient Minoan palace of Knossos in Crete depict roses clearly identifiable as *Rosa damascena*. They date, according to historians, from two thousands years before the birth of Christ. A variety of Damask was extensively cultivated— in heated 'green-houses'—by the Romans of the imperial Caesars to provide fragrant flowers for ceremonial festivals. It is the fragrance we have today in the red hybrid teas of *damascena* lineage. But with it has come, unfortunately, the characteristic tendency to weak-stemmed blooms (the hanging head of Ena Harkness again) and the 'blueing' of the flowers as they age.

Several fine damask roses are available for use in the shrub gardens of today. One of them, Omar Khayyam, a typically-scented light pink, has a romantic story all its own. For Omar Khayyam is the variety that was rescued from a weed-choked death on a graveside at Woodbridge churchyard in the county of Suffolk. It was found there, dwindling into possible extinction, when the grave of Edward FitzGerald, the man who translated Omar Khayyam into English, was renovated just after the Second World War. Intended to protect the precious plant was a wire cage, on which was a plaque that bore this inscription:

'This rose tree, raised in Kew Gardens from seed brought by William Simpson, artist and traveller, from the grave of Omar Khayyam at Nashipur, was planted by a few admirers of Edward FitzGerald in the name of the Omar Khayyam Club, October 7, 1893.'

The plant was rescued, a few budding eyes taken from it to ensure continuance of the variety, and there are now sufficient Omar Khayyams in existence for anyone who cares to have the variety in his own gardens.

A meandering butterfly or perhaps a honey bee effected a chance pollination between a *Rosa damascena* and a *Rosa chinensis*—the China rose—among plants of these species serving as a windbreak on the Ile de Bourbon in France. It gave us the Bourbon roses, still among the most beautiful of shrubs. From the Bourbons were bred the hybrid perpetuals which delighted gardeners of the late 1800s by growing happily where so many of the inherently delicate tea roses failed. The teas and the perpetuals were crossed to produce the hybrid teas.

In a catalogue issued in 1884 by the famous old firm of William Paul and Sons, of Cheshunt, Hertfordshire, no fewer than 800 named varieties of hybrid perpetuals are listed. Today, only Frau Karl Druschki, with its statuesque white blooms, and the pink Mrs John Laing would be generally considered as space-worthy hybrid perpetuals—and both these had yet to come on the scene when William Paul published his gigantic list.

Both could well find a place in a modern representative shrub garden and, for myself, I would not like to be without the two species *Rosa foetida*, and *Rosa foetida bicolor*—often known as the Austrian Briar and the Austrian Copper, quite irrationally since both come from Asia Minor. Both need to be watched for black spot, but the effort is worthwhile since they are attractive mid-summer fountains of highly-scented blossoms. The bicolor variety, deep amber-bronze on the upper surface of its petals with a deep golden-yellow reverse, is of added interest because it is the only known bicolor among species roses. The Tudors knew both these varieties. More recently Meilland used the bicolor to help give us the peerless Peace.

The rugosas, natives of Japan, have been developed into some superb varieties. None are more attractive, in my opinion, than two with quaint frilled petals. They are the red F. J. Grootendorst and its even more appealing sport known simply as Pink Grooten-dorst. From July onwards, these are repeatedly in bloom.

If a shrub border is to be complete, it should include at least one specimen of *centifolia*, the rose of a hundred petals, beloved by the ancients but denigrated by some people today as a 'cabbage rose'. Misguidedly, the impression has been allowed to arise that any rose with a full, rather loose centre, like Caroline Testout, for instance, must be a 'cabbage rose'. In truth, only varieties of *centifolia* are entitled to be described as cabbage roses, and this term, as it was originally applied, was intended as praise.

To them we owe the moss roses, a much more recent group even though they are known to have existed since the early eighteenth century. Moss roses are mutations or natural sports of *centifolia*. The mossing is due to the development of minute hairs on the calyx, flower stems, and leaves. These become even more pro-nounced as breeders began their work of selection and hybridisa-tion. And what caused the moss to appear in the first place? The modern theory is that the appearance of the hairs was a natural protection against heat—which possibly occurred, in the first place, in Italy. To my mind the delightful, almost youthful moss variety, Nuits de Young, originated in 1850, should be in any top twelve collection of shrub roses. It has black-velvet flowers, each with a cluster of golden anthers, backed by a mass of chestnut brown.

At the end of the list which follows, I was almost tempted to add one more, an *alba* rose called Cuisse de Nymphe Emu, roughly translated as the Thigh of the Passionate Nymph. It is blush pink. I decided to keep her out of it—her performance is less than her promise.

ALOHA: cl. HT; United States, 1949, Boerner; Mercedes Gallart (cl. HT) ×The New Dawn (PFC); flowers large (3½ in.), 55–60 petals, cupped, rose pink, shading to coral with deeper reverse; fragrant, free and continuous-flowering; foliage leathery, dark green. A pillar rose reaching 6 to 7 ft.—but better as a free-growing shrub. Requires little pruning.

BALLERINA: h. musk; England, 1937, Bentall; small single soft pink and white flowers, in big open trusses; continuously in bloom; foliage pale green, somewhat sparse; height, no more than 4 ft., which makes it one of the front of the border shrubs and a valuable asset there.

BERLIN: h. musk; Germany, 1950, Kordes; Eva (h. musk) ×Peace (HT); brilliant orange scarlet single flowers in profusion (3 in. across); scented; of floribunda habit, reaching 5 ft. tall. Very showy specimen.

CHINATOWN: fl.; Denmark, 1963, Poulsen; Columbine (fl.) ×Clare Grammerstorf (fl.); blooms large (4 in.), full, freely-produced in small clusters; yellow, sometimes edged pink, like a smaller Peace; markedly fragrant; foliage mid-green, leathery; growth tall, bushy, to 5½ ft. Gold Medal, Britain, 1962.

59 COCKTAIL: PFC sh.-type; France, 1957, Meilland; Independence (fl.) ×Orange Triumph (fl.) ×Phyllis Bide (*H. rugosa*); medium-sized flowers, single, 5 petals, geranium red on yellow base, in clusters; free-growing to 5½ ft. but will reach 8 ft. as climber or pillar rose in warmer conditions; foliage glossy, mid-green. Doesn't mind rain but intolerant of hard frost.

CORNELIA: h. musk; Britain, 1925, Pemberton; apricot yellow, flushed pink, small flowers in very large trusses; very fragrant; vigorous, spreading, to 6 ft.

60 DOROTHY WHEATCROFT: fl.; Germany, 1960, Tantau; large blooms (3½ in.), attractive semi-double, produced in massive clusters. I have seen one with more than 80 blooms on the head; Orient red, with darker shadings; slightly fragrant; growth to 6½ ft., sturdy and upright. Gold Medal, Britain, 1961.

EVA: h. musk; Germany, 1933, Kordes; Robin Hood (h. musk) ×J. C. Thornton (HT); single flowers, carmine red with white eye, produced in large trusses; free and persistent flowering; growth vigorous and spreading, 6 ft. tall and as much across.

FIRST CHOICE: fl.; England, 1958, Morse; Masquerade (fl.) × Sultane (HT); large (5 in.) single flowers, 7 petals, in trusses; brilliant

Frühlingsgold (*photos Graham Thomas and Downward*)

Mme Pierre Oger and
La Reine Victoria (*photo Graham Thomas*)

Frühlingsmorgen (*photos Graham Thomas*)

Tour de Malakoff
(*photo Graham Thomas*)

Old Blush (*photo Graham Thomas*)

Miniatures
1. June Time
2. Baby Masquerade
3. Little Buckaroo
4. Josephine Wheatcroft
5. Baby Darling
6. Pour Toi
7. Purple Elf

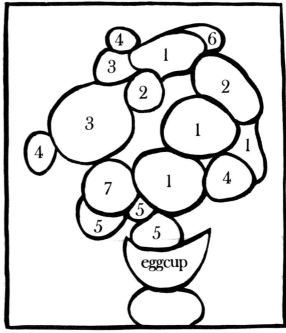

orange-scarlet, surrounding yellow centres; free, repeat-flowering; growth spreading to 5 ft.; foliage dark green, leathery. An attractive specimen tree.

FELICIA: h. musk; Britain, 1928, Pemberton; Trier (rugosa) ×Ophelia (HT); small blooms, salmon pink, shading to blush and ivory, very freely produced on long branching sprays; very fragrant; height to 6 ft., spreading proportionately; recurrent-flowering.

F. J. GROOTENDORST: rugosa sh.; Holland, 1918, de Goey; *R.* rugosa ×unnamed dwarf polyantha; small crimson flowers, edges frilled like a pink, in clusters; profuse and recurrent; leathery, wrinkled, mid-green foliage; rather straggling habit, 6 ft. tall, spreading.

FRED LOADS: fl.; England, 1967, R. Holmes; Orange Sensation (fl.) × Dorothy Wheatcroft; large (4 in.) single blooms, in heads more than 18 in. wide; light vermilion, similar to Anna Wheatcroft; fragrant; foliage light green, semi-glossy; growth vigorous and upright to 5½ ft. Gold Medal, Britain, 1967.

FRUHLINGSGOLD: *H. spinosissima*; Germany, 1937, Kordes; Joanna   **61** Hill (HT) ×*R. spinosissima hispida*; pointed buds opening to profuse large (3 in.) single flowers; very fragrant, golden yellow; foliage large, soft green; growth vigorous, spreading and bushy to 7 ft.; definitely needs room.

FRUHLINGSMORGEN: *H. spinosissima*; Germany, 1942, Kordes;   **62** medium-sized (2½ in.) single blooms, with yellow centre, showing maroon stamens; very free May–June; some repeat later; foliage dark green, leathery; growth to 6½ ft., with long branching stems freely produced.

HUNTER: h. musk; England, 1961, Mattock; double bright crimson flowers, borne the full length of long widely-arching stems; flowers freely, summer and autumn. Height to 6 ft., bushy.

JOSEPH'S COAT: sh. HT type; United States, 1964, Armstrong and Swim; Buccaneer (HT) ×Circus (fl.); large (3 in.), double, yellow and red multi-coloured flowers in clusters; free and recurrent; growth upright, vigorous, to 6 ft.; foliage light green, leathery. Gold Medal, France, Bagatelle, 1964.

LADY SONIA: h. musk; England, 1961, Mattock; Grandmaster (h. musk) ×Doreen (HT); large flowers (3½ in.), semi-double, 20 petals, of deep buttercup yellow, splashed with orange. Growth vigorous and spreading to 6 ft. A valuable modern introduction.

LAVENDER LASSIE: h. musk; Germany, 1960, Kordes; large (3 in.), double, very fragrant lilac and pink flowers in large clusters; profuse, recurrent bloom; growth vigorous, tall, well-branched.

MARCHENLAND: fl.; Germany, 1951, Tantau; Swantje (fl.) × Hamburg (sh.); large (4 in.), semi-double flowers, rose-tinted salmon, 17 petals, in clusters of 40 or more; very free-flowering; foliage dark green, glossy; growth vigorous and spreading.

NEVADA; (*H. moyesii*): Spain, 1927, Dot; reported to be a hybrid of **La Giralda** (HT) × *R. moyesii*. Some doubts exist and the Americans suggest that *R. moyesii gargesii*, a tetraploid form of *moyesii*, may have been the species used. Bud ovoid, pale pink, opening to large white single flowers, 5 in. across, with prominent golden stamens; profuse bloom, recurrent; growth vigorous and bushy to 7 ft. A handsome specimen.

PENELOPE: h. musk; Britain, 1924, Pemberton; unnamed seedling × Ophelia (HT); pale pink, shaded salmon; small blooms in clusters; free-flowering, recurrent; scented. Growth shrubby, to 5 ft., spreading. Gold Medal, Britain, 1925.

PINK GROOTENDORST: rugosa sh.; Holland, 1923, Grootendorst; pink sport from F. J. Grootendorst (which see). Flowers bright pink, frilled; otherwise similar to the parent variety.

SPARRIESHOOP: sh., HT-type; Germany, 1953, Kordes; Baby Chateau fl.) ×Else Poulsen (fl.) × Magnifica (*R. rubiginosa*); long pointed buds, opening to large (4 in.) flowers of about 30 petals; light pink; highly fragrant; foliage leathery, dark green; height 5 ft.; vigorous and bushy; bloom profuse but intermittent. A beautiful variety.

UNCLE WALTER: HT sh.; Ireland, 1963, McGredy; Brilliant (HT) × Heidelberg (sh.); large blooms (5 in.), about 30 petals, scarlet-crimson with deeper shadings; perfectly formed with high-pointed centres; very free-flowering; foliage dark green, glossy, with copper shadings; height to 6 ft., tall and upright. Certificate of Merit, Britain, 1963.

VANITY: h. musk; Britain, 1920, Pemberton; Chateau de Clos Vougeot (HT) × unnamed seedling; deep carmine single blooms (3 in. across), in large clusters; free and continuous-flowering; very vigorous to 8 ft. or more.

WILHLEM (syn. Skyrocket): h. musk; Germany, 1934, Kordes; Robin Hood (h. musk) × J. C. Thornton (HT). A full brother, a year younger, to Eva; deep-red semi-double flowers in large clusters, freely borne. Even more vigorous than Eva, 10 ft. and the same across. A very fine shrub.

R. alba: GREAT MAIDEN'S BLUSH; a soft pink to represent a group that is nominally white. Raised at Kew in 1797, this is a magnificent variety, spanning 6 to 8 ft., with large flowers, full and fragrant.

R. alba semi-plena: THE WHITE ROSE OF YORK; white, small, semi-double flowers produced freely in a four-week crop lasting from mid-June to mid-July. Vigorous bushes to 8 ft., with grey-green foliage characteristic of the type.

R. banksiae var. *lutea:* THE YELLOW BANKSIAN ROSE; introduced in 1824, and bearing masses of small double yellow rosette-shaped blooms. This one is a climber that you can happily use to cover and smother an old tree stump—it grows to 30 ft. or more. Go easy on the pruning—it bears its flowers on the sub-laterals, side-shoots from the side-shoots off the main stem.

R. bourboniana, the BOURBON ROSE.

BOULE DE NEIGE; raised in France by Lacharme in 1867; creamy white edged pink, flowers full and round; heavily fragrant; deep green, glossy foliage; height and girth to 5 ft. I have seen it used as an exceptionally beautiful hedge.

COMMANDANT BEAUREPAIRE; 1874 (syn. Panachée d'Angres); a startler, incurved petals, with alternate stripes of pink, lilac, purple and deep maroon on a crimson base. Plenty of bloom in summer; not so much later but one you just can't miss. Strong, bushy grower to 5 ft. or more.

HONORINE DE BRABANT; introduced 1880; pale lilac with deeper shadings; full flowers repeating well in the autumn. Growth strong and vigorous—again to 5 ft.

LA REINE VICTORIA; 1872; lilac pink, full-petalled and continuous-flowering. A wonderful scent—and a sturdy six-footer. One of the best.

62

LOUISE ODIER; an 1851 introduction in soft pink-tinted lilac, with flowers of camellia-shape. Repeat-flowering and highly fragrant. Grows to 6 ft. proportions.

MME ISAAC PEREIRE; 1881; purplish crimson, large, loosely-formed blooms with exquisite fragrance. Will make an 8 ft. free-growing shrub or stretch to 10 ft. if trained against a wall.

62 MME PIERRE OGER; 1878; rosy violet shadings over a cream base. A sport from La Reine Victoria. Free intermittent flowering and fragrant. Growth slender and erect to 5 ft.

VARIEGATA DI BOLOGNA; 1909; a late arrival but an interesting one. Globular white flowers with deep-crimson stripes. Highly fragrant. Very free summer-flowering with some autumn repeat. Height to 6 ft.

ZEHIRINE DROUHIN; 1868; see climbing rose section. This one can still hold its own with the moderns.

R. centifolia. The best are:

DE MEAUX, introduced 1814; one for the front of the shrub border, growing no more than 3 ft. tall. Slender, erect growth with pom-poms of pale-pink flowers, opening early as though to herald the whole shrub rose pageant.

FANTIN LATOUR; a larger proportioned beauty, with masses of full shell-pink flowers much to the delight of the old floral artists. They last over a long period, too. Growth is vigorous to 5 ft.

63 TOUR DE MALAKOFF, introduced 1856; this one is as sprawling as Petite de Hollande is compact, to make a loose, somewhat untidy-looking bush at least 5 ft. tall. But those flowers of magenta and mauve, stained with purple and a smoky grey are worthy any temporary inconvenience its stretching limbs may cause.

UNIQUE BLANCHE, so-called because it lasts a full month longer in flower than the rest of this group. Also named White Provence, it was found growing in a shopkeeper's garden in Suffolk in 1775.

R. centifolia var. *muscosa*, is the Moss Rose. Best are:

BLANCHE MOREAU, introduced 1880; paper-white, full, cupped flowers with brown moss. Highly fragrant; growth to 4 ft.

CAPT. JOHN INGRAM; 1856; red purple, with lilac centre, against dark-red moss; summer-flowering only; vigorous grower to 4 ft.

COMMON MOSS (syn. Old Pink Moss, Pink Moss, Communis); soft pink, well-mossed buds opening flat, full and very fragrant. Height to 4 ft. and a real veteran, dating from 1727.

NUITS DE YOUNG, 1852; my favourite among them all. Deep maroon purple, at times almost black flowers, showing golden stamens against a brown moss. Each one a gem and so many of them. Vigorous, slender grower to 4½ ft.

WILLIAM LOBB, 1855; purple-magenta flowers fading to lilac grey; well-mossed and highly fragrant. But this one is not for the first row of the chorus, it grows to 7 ft. or more.

R. chinensis:

CRAMOISIE SUPERIEURE, 1832; constantly repeating dark crimson medium sized flowers in large clusters; moderately vigorous.

GLOIRE DES ROSOMANES (syn. Ragged Robin); introduced 1825; glowing crimson in large clusters, perpetual-flowering. Used in some parts of the United States as an understock for budding.

OLD BLUSH, 1796 (syn. the Common Monthly Rose); a neat little shrub, bearing masses of medium-sized, full flowers in summer and autumn. Old-time gardeners considered it formed new displays of bloom every month, hence the synonym. Thought to have been the original variety, introduced to Europe and America, from China, by way of India, in the eighteenth century.

R. damascena: the Damask rose:

MME HARDY, 1832; pure white, occasionally tinted the faintest blush; large full flowers with typically incurved centre petals; very fragrant, making a large bush to 5 ft.

OMAR KHAYYAM; light pink, incurving centre petals; heavily scented. The rose brought to England from old Omar's grave in India.

Var. *versicolor:* THE YORK AND LANCASTER ROSE; said, without foundation in fact, to be the rose symbolising the reunion of the warring factions in the Wars of the Roses. Semi-double flowers, loosely-formed, striped white and pink. Not very vigorous for a 4-ft. bush, it requires light pruning immediately after flowering to encourage development of flowering shoots for the following season.

R. foetida: misnamed the Austrian Briar. Known to have been brought to England from Asia Minor and the Middle East in the middle 1500s. Single yellow flowers borne profusely, especially in warmer districts. Growth to 5 ft. under British conditions.

R. foetida bicolor (syn. the Austrian Copper), also a misnomer. To French-men it is the Capucine Rose. Orange copper with yellow reverse, it is similar in other respects to *foetida*, from which it is thought to have sported.

R. foetida persiana, the Persian Yellow. Another *foetida* sport, this one with double-yellow flowers, re-introduced to England from Persia in 1837. This is the rose Pernet-Ducher used to develop the pernetianas, with their 'new' orange and flame colourings.

R. gallica, the Apothecary's Rose, one of our earliest-known species to which many of our moderns owe their heritage. Mostly summer-flowering, very fragrant, making compact bushes to 3½ ft.

BELLE DE CRECY; pink, shaded mauve, incurving petals, very few thorns.

CARDINAL DE RICHELIEU; 1840: violet purple, small, very fragrant flowers on a dense bush; introduced by Laffay, the old French hybridist who gave us so many of the moss roses, this is one of the later additions to the Gallica range. Said to be almost identical to the famous old Blue Rose of the Arabs.

CHARLES DE MILLS; quartered crimson and purple flowers, with re-flexing petals. Growing to 5 ft., rather more lusty than most of its type.

DU MAITRE d'ECOLE; carmine-to-mauve flowers, exceptionally fra-grant, and larger than most gallicas. Strong grower to 4 ft.

TUSCANY; one of the oldest varieties, deep purple semi-double flowers on a vigorous bush. Used extensively by the old hybridists in the develop-ment of the red hybrid perpetuals.

Var. *versicolor* or *R. mundi*. A natural sport from the true *gallica* types, with large semi-double crimson blooms striped pink and white, this is said to be the rose named after Fair Rosamund, mistress of England's King Henry the Second.

R. highdownensis: one of our most attractive shrub species, developed in 1928 at Highdown, in Sussex, as a seedling from *R. moyesii*. Bears masses of deep pink single flowers in summer, to be followed by long bottle-shaped scarlet heps. Very vigorous and branching to 10 ft., this is altogether one of the shrub garden's show-pieces.

R. hugonis: another species not to be missed. The Golden Rose of China, sent to Europe by the French missionary Peter Hugo in 1899. Bears masses of single yellow flowers on long sweeping branches with delicate, almost fern-like foliage. Height to 6 ft., but it is broader than it is tall.

R. moyesii: brought from Western China in 1894, this one is a giant, soaring up to 10 ft. or more. Bright deep red single flowers, followed by large bottle-shaped heps, 3 in. long. The variety Geranium is a seedling from the parent type, with bright scarlet flowers and even larger fruits, but is rather less vigorous in growth.

R. rubiginosa: the Eglantines or sweet briars, one of England's native roses, all with typically-scented foliage. Garden hybrids, developed by Lord Penzance in the 1890's, include these outstanding varieties:

AMY ROBSART; rose pink, large semi-double flowers, followed by scarlet heps; very vigorous to 8 ft.

ANN OF GERSTEIN; dark crimson single flowers; scarlet heps; 8 ft.

LADY PENZANCE; copper, with yellow centre, growing to 6 ft.

LORD PENZANCE; fawn yellow single flowers in clusters on long, strong stems. Exceptionally vigorous to 10 ft. or more.

MEG MERRILEES; bright crimson single; another strong grower to 10 ft.

R. rugosa: the Japanese species, usually covered in masses of short, needle-sharp thorns, commercially used as an understock for standard roses. Outstanding older varieties are:

BLANC DOUBLE de COUBERT; 1892: double sport from *R. rugosa alba*; pure white, large semi-double, very fragrant; a handsome bush to 6 ft.

CONRAD FERDINAND MEYER; 1899: silvery-pink flowers, often of exhibition size and quality, on strong stems often more than 8 ft. long. Little repeat-flowering after the summer flush but one of the classic shrubs.

FRAU DAGMAR HASTRUP; clear rose-pink single flowers, continuously produced in great profusion; large scarlet heps; growth vigorous to 4 ft.

MRS ANTHONY WATERER; 1898: large purplish-crimson semi-double flowers, with some repeat bloom in autumn; vigorous to 4 ft. The hybrid perpetual Général Jacqueminot is in its pedigree, which probably accounts for its wonderful fragrance.

PARFUM de l'HAY; 1903: another cross between Général Jacqueminot and the species; cherry-crimson medium-sized blooms, again strongly fragrant; a shorter grower, to 3 ft., but lacking nothing in robustness.

ROSERIE de l'HAY; purplish crimson, very large, loosely-formed flowers continuously produced; highly fragrant; growth to 7 ft. One of our finest shrubs.

R. spinosissima. The Scotch Rose. In addition to the modern hybrids developed by Kordes, there is:

STANWELL PERPETUAL: a dense, rather prickly shrub, found in a garden at Stanwell, Middlesex in 1838. Probably a chance hybrid, it bears white 3-in. flowers, sometimes shaded pink, persistently throughout the season. Very vigorous to 4 ft.

R. xanthina, var. *spontanea*. CANARY BIRD. A shrub native to China and North Korea. Canary Bird bears rich yellow single flowers, $2\frac{1}{2}$ in. across, on graceful, long, arching stems in early summer. Both this, and the double yellow form, *R. xanthina* var. *slingeri*, are among our most decorative garden shrubs. Growth extremely vigorous to 6 ft.

If you want a shrub rose for the sake of its wonderfully decorative foliage, I suggest *R. omeiansis pteracantha*, a species brought from China in 1890. It bears curious little four-petalled single flowers in spring but its decorative value lies in its small, fern-like leaves and sharp broad, translucent, ruby-red thorns. It grows to 15 ft. but must be pruned hard to ensure plenty of those red-thorned shoots so eagerly sought by floral decorators.

Miniatures

I was amused when I read 'Dorothy Wheatcroft is too tall for the average-sized bed', and also when I found Josephine Wheatcroft described as the perfect miniature. For Dorothy Wheatcroft is my wife; Josephine our daughter. The descriptions fit the roses, but certainly not their real life namesakes. For Dorothy is certainly no giant, and Josephine is taller than her mother.

But it is of Dorothy and Josephine the roses that I am thinking now and especially of Josephine. For of all the miniatures, this one surely is the finest. Imagine a bouquet of classically-shaped, high-centred, pure deep-yellow hybrid tea blooms; each one of them small enough to slip through any woman's wedding ring. There you have Josephine, queen of the Lilliputians.

I had the pleasure of naming her, when the real-life Josephine was still a toddler in the nursery, because I introduced this new miniature gem into England. Josephine Wheatcroft is, in fact, only a synonym. In Spain, the country of her birth, she was christened Rosina. She came from Pedro Dot, that doyen of hybridists, who has given the world a host of wonderful roses, from the luxuriant, impressive shrub Nevada to the latest 'blue' novelty, Godfrey Winn. Most notably, over recent years, he has met with considerable success with his miniatures. And Rosina, or Josephine, was one of the first of his family.

Now while Pedro, long past the age when lesser men would have

M

thought of retiring, was busy hybridising in the Iberian sun, on his nursery just outside Madrid, my old friend John de Vink was just as successfully raising and lowering his drawbridge in Holland. John is the man who really pioneered the return of the miniatures —in fact, they are a much older class than is generally realised— and he really has a drawbridge. His nursery, the whole half-acre of it, is on a tiny canal-surrounded island near Boskoop. He has to lower the drawbridge each day to get to work; raise it when he leaves. It is scarcely an island in the sun, but there, under glass, John has managed to create his thimble-sized masterpieces.

I have said miniature roses are no new innovation, even though they have never enjoyed anything like their present popularity. The first of them, in fact, was brought to Britain in the early 1800s; a child of the East, said to have originated in Japan as a crossing from the climbing multiflora species and to have been dwarfed by traditional Japanese bonsai methods. It was called here the Dwarf Pink China Rose. British gardeners apparently weren't particularly interested. The French were. They used Dwarf Pink China to produce several new miniatures, none of them more than six inches tall, in the 1820s. Redouté, master portrayer of the rose in his classical prints, is said to have turned his artistic hand to hybridising and even to have raised, in 1821, one of the earliest-known true miniatures.

But the craze for the tiny tots seems to have died with Napoleon. Miniature roses dropped out of cultivation for a hundred years. They might, indeed, have been lost to the world altogether had not a certain Dr Roulet, in 1918, found one of them growing in a tiny pot on a cottage windowsill near Onnen, in Switzerland. He was told it had been in the same family's possession, growing there as a curiosity of considerable local repute, for more than one hundred years. Roulet took his find, now believed to be the old variety Pompon de Paris, to a Swiss nurseryman, who put it back into propagation and re-christened it *Rosa rouletti*, after the worthy doctor whom he thought was the discoverer of a new race. It is by the name *Rosa rouletti* that roses of this type are botanically known today.

Now this is where my old friend John de Vink found his place in history. Quick to appreciate the commercial possibilities of these midget roses that are, in every way, perfect miniatures of their

Pedro Dot.

John de Vink.

garden-sized counterparts, he obtained a few specimens of *Rosa rouletti* and set about crossing them with the polyantha pom-pom Gloria Mundi, a low-growing variety which carries its full, yet only button sized, bright orange-scarlet flowers in tight clusters. The first of the cross to bloom was a delightful one bearing masses of crimson, white-centred blooms, which de Vink called Peon.

And it was this Peon, the one plant then in flower, that the late Robert Pyle, (then head of the vast Conard-Pyle Rose Company of Philadelphia), taking a working holiday in Holland, bought, in its tiny pot, to take back to America. Back home, Bob Pyle propagated it, re-christened it Tom Thumb and, in 1936, obtained a patent for it as the forerunner of a new race of midget roses. His introduction received such quick popularity that, within a year of first offering it for sale, Conard-Pyle had to withdraw it from their lists while they worked up sufficient stocks to meet a backlog of orders. Tom Thumb was a winner from the start.

John de Vink had set the pattern for the new mini-fashion. With the money he got from Pyle, he built a new greenhouse on his half-acre of land and from under its roof, using Tom Thumb to cross with the polyantha Ellen Poulsen, he produced a succession of mini-beauties; Pixie, Midget, and an exquisitely-scented master-piece called Sweet Fairy. Then, from him, came Bo Peep, Red Imp (synonym Maid Marion) and Baby Bunting. And so it has gone on. John de Vink and Pedro Dot in Europe; Ralph Moore breeding in America, have between them dominated the world of the Lilliputians. Pedro Dot's miniatures are largely of hybrid tea shape; he has used the deep-golden Spek's Yellow in breeding many of them. John de Vink's productions are characterised by their smaller, rounder flowers. But John's achievement is that he has kept his introductions true miniatures. Some, from other raisers, are now topping eighteen inches or more; and that, for me, appears to be growing out of the class.

Because I believe that field production of miniatures—budding them in the open on to small *canina* briars—tends to increase the size of all members of the race, we are now raising all of ours under glass. But don't be misled by that. If you decide to adopt these babies, don't mollycoddle them. For they are as hardy as any hybrid tea or floribunda growing in the garden.

Ralph Moore.

The late Robert Pyle
with a specimen shrub
of *R. alba*.

BABY BETSY McCALL: Moore, America, 1960; HT-type flowers of pearly pink, repeated all summer; 8 in. tall.

BABY BUNTING: de Vink, Holland, 1954; light magenta flowers, 20 petals, showing stamens; 8 in. tall; fragrant.

BABY CRIMSON (syn. Perla de Alcanada, Wheatcroft's Baby Crimson): Dot, Spain, 1944; rose-red flowers the size of a sixpence; 7 in. tall; one of the earliest introductions, still one of the best.

64 BABY DARLING: Moore, America, 1964; full double flowers, 20 petals of orange apricot; 12 in.

BABY GOLD STAR (syn. Baby Gold): Dot, Spain, 1940; perfect HT-shaped flowers of 40 petals, golden yellow flushed apricot; 13 in.

64 BABY MASQUARADE: Tantau, Germany, 1956; a Tom Thumb × Masquerade cross, with all Masquerade's colours and characteristics in miniature; 12 in.

BAMBINO: Dot, Spain, 1953; pink sport of Perla de Alcanada; like a baby Mischief; 12 in.

CORALIN (syn. Carolin, Carolyn, Karolyn): Dot, Spain, 1953; full double, 40 petals, coral shaded orange; a colour break and one of Dot's best; 8 in.

DWARF KING: Kordes, Germany, 1957; another Tom Thumb cross; fragrant, classically-shaped carmine flowers, 25 petals; very free; 9 in.

ELEANOR: Moore, America, 1960; long pointed pink buds, 25 petals, resembling a tiny Queen Elizabeth; 12 in.

ELF (syn. Red Elf): de Vink, Holland, 1940; dark crimson and the smallest of them all; blooms just half an inch across; plant only 4 in. high; a real little beauty; slightly fragrant, too.

64 JOSEPHINE WHEATCROFT (syn. Rosina): Dot, Spain, 1950; golden sunflower-yellow flowers of perfect shape, 16 petals, in clusters; fragrant; growth to 15 in.

64 JUNE TIME: Moore, America, 1963; flowers of 75 petals, light pink, darker on the reverse; a little button-bush, growing to 10 in.; delightful.

LITTLE BUCKAROO: Moore, America, 1956; long lasting bright-red **64** flowers, 23 petals; fresh apple fragrance; growth to 15 in.

LITTLE FLIRT: Moore, America, 1961; flowers like a miniature Tzigane, orange red, with yellow reverse; 45 petals; slight fragrance; 12 in.

MIDGET: de Vink, Holland, 1941; half-inch blooms of 20 petals, crimson carmine, with a white eye; very attractive fern-like foliage; 8 in.

MON PETIT: Dot, Spain, 1947; light-red blooms, 80 petals; obtained by a direct cross from the old Pompon de Paris; 8 in.

NEW PENNY: Moore, America, 1962; salmon-orange semi-double flowers (20 petals) in profusion; 10 in.

POUR TOI (syn. Para Ti, Wendy, For You); Dot, Spain, 1946; creamy **64** yellow, of perfect shape, 15 petals; 17 in.

PRESUMIDA (syn. Peter Pan, Baby Talisman): Dot, Spain, 1948; apricot-peach shading to white; very free; 9 in.

PURPLE ELF: Moore, America, 1963; small, double flowers, 50 petals, **64** fuchsia to cyclamen-purple; very bushy growth to 12 in.

RED IMP (syn. Maid Marion, Mon Tresor): de Vink, Holland, 1951; deep-crimson flowers three-quarters in. across, 55 petals, opening flat but always delightful; 9 in.

SCARLET GEM (syn. Scarlet Pimpernel): Meilland, France, 1961; one-inch orange-scarlet blooms of 60 tiny petals; has the floribundas Moulin Rouge and Fashion in its pedigree; 15 in.

SWEET FAIRY: de Vink, Holland, 1946; apple-blossom pink flowers. three-quarters in. diameter, in profusion and also gloriously scented; named among America's 'Top Twenty' roses of all kinds in 1960, the first miniature ever to rate such distinction.

TOM THUMB (syn. Peon): de Vink, Holland, 1936; the daddy of them all; a mass of blooms, little more than half in. across, of 40 tightly-packed petals; crimson red, with white centres; 5 in.

Index

INDEX OF VARIETIES

(Bold Figures indicate colour plates)

INDEX OF NAMES AND PLACES

(Bold figures indicate colour plates)

Hole, Dean Samuel, 110, 111, 112, 117
Holstein, Germany, 23
Horstmann, Adolf, nursery, **8**
Howard, Frederick, 88
Howard and Swim, 88
Howard Rose Company, 90

International Registration Authority 138
Ile de Bourbon, France, 165

Jackson and Perkins, 30, 53, 54, 60, 61, 138, 151
Jenner, Robert, 57
Jepson, Helen, 60

Kew Gardens, London, 66, 67, 164, 165
Klimenko, Vera, 121
Knossos, Crete, 165
Kordes and Krause, 48
Kordes, Hermann, 52
Kordes, Reimar, 48, 52
Kordes, roses of, 12, 34, 38, 43, 55, 62, 69, 90, 91, 161
Kordes Wilhelm, **12, 20**, 22, 33, 34, 46–52, 47, 68, 88

Krause, Max, 46, 49
Kvistogaard, Denmark, 136

Lambert, Peter, 138
Lammerts, Dr. W. E., 24, 25, 90
Le Grice, Edward, 61, 62, 71
Lens, Louis, 62
Lindquist, Robert, 90, 91, 92
Livermore, California, 24
Los Angeles, 25
Lyons, France, 26, 53

Madrid, Spain, 53, 54, 55
Malcolm, Mr., 150
Mallerin, roses of, 62
McFarland, *Modern Roses*, 84, 121
McGredy, roses of, 36, 44, 56, 60, 61, 70, 71, 137, 161
Meilland, Alain, 27
Meilland, Antoine ('Papa'), **14**, 27
Meilland, Francis, 27, 28, 38, 88, 90
Meilland, roses of, 30, 31, 34, 44, 55, 61, 62, 73, 91, 121, 166
Modern Roses, see McFarland
Moore Ralph, 180, 181
Morse, Ernest, 49

Nabonnand, Paul, 148
Newark, New Jersey, 53
Nicholas, J. H., 138
Norman, Albert, 32, 64
North Walsham, 61
Nottingham, 117

Omar Khayyam, 165
Onnen, Switzerland, 178

Paris, 34
Park, Bertram, 91
Paul, William & Sons, 41, 166
Pernet-Ducher, Joseph, 34, 41, 42, 43, 65
Portland, Oregon, 53, 137
Poulsen, D. T., 91, 136, 137
Poulsen, Svend, 137
Princess Mary's Rose Border, Royal National Rose Society, **34**
Pyle, Robert, 180, 181

Queen Elizabeth II, 25
Queen Mary's Rose Garden, Regents' Park, **31, 33**, 53, 116
Queen Victoria, 57

Raffel, Frank, 61
Redouté, 178
Regents' Park, London, 25, 53
Robinson, Herbert, 43, 49
Rose Annual, 26, 46, 69, 91
Roulet, Dr, 178
Roussel, M., 39
Rousselet, M., 39
Rowley, Gordon, 69
Royal Horticultural Society, 23
Royal National Rose Society, **32, 34**, 13, 17, 24, 25, 29, 34, 36, 40, 43, 53, 56, 57, 83, 85, 88, 90, 110, 116, 117, 121, 122, 151
Ruddington, England, 50

Sanday of Bristol, 61
St. Alban's, England, 13, 53, 91, 116
San Francisco, California, 26
Sangerhausen, Germany, 68
Simpson, William, 165
Smith, Robert, 58
Southill Park, England, 149, 150
Sparrieshoop, Germany, 49
Spry, Constance, 60
Sutter's Creek, America, 88
Swim, Herbert, 44, 88, 89, 90